What homebrewers are saying about this book:

"It is clear, concise, easy to understand and to follow. A must for beginner and seasoned homebrewers."

– Frank Mengler

"Some of the tips are a bit off the wall, but that's what homebrewing is all about. I've never heard of using marbles — I can't wait to give that one a try."

– Jim Trautwein (*HomeBrewer's Software*)

"It fills a great niche."

– Charlie Papazian, President, *Association of Brewers*

"It was fun reading. I especially enjoyed the humour that you were able to mingle with the tips."

– Pamela Gammans (*NEPT*)

"Mr. Weisberg's book is not only helpful, but entertaining, too. People who understand that there is no definitive book on homebrewing will add this collection to their library and I guarantee it will be used."

– Christopher J. Heatley

"Very good—nice humor. Very user friendly."

– Jeff Handley, *Handley's Homebrewing*

"*50 Great Homebrewing Tips* packs more quality brewing info than books twice its size.... Weisberg gets four stars, I can't wait for the next edition!"

– Donald Gosselin, President/CEO, *Yankee Brew News*

W9-BIT-538

50 Great Homebrewing Tips

Practical brewing tips and techniques
to help beginning homebrewers
brew the perfect pint!

by DAVID WEISBERG

Lampman Brewing Publications
P.O. Box 684
Peterborough, New Hampshire 03458-0684
(603) 827-3432

50 Great Homebrewing Tips

Practical tips and techniques to help beginning homebrewers brew the perfect pint!

Cover design by James Fletcher (Times Design, Peterborough, NH)

Line drawings by Barbara Bitzer-Richter

Graphic assistance by NEPT (Keene, NH)

Photographs by David Weisberg

Label illustrations by Julie Weisberg

Copyright ©1994 and 1995 by David A. Weisberg

Published by: **Lampman Brewing Publications**

P.O. Box 684, Peterborough, NH 03458-0684 U.S.A.

First Printing 1994

Second Printing 1995, revised

Third Printing 1995, completely revised

ISBN 0-9642746-2-0 Softcover.

Printed in the United States of America by Bradford and Bigelow, Inc.

Dedication

To my parents who encouraged me in all areas at an early age. In whatever I did, they were behind me 100 percent.

And to my wife, Julie, who continues to encourage me. Thanks for your help and understanding during the writing and editing of this book. Your insight to beer appreciation has also helped this endeavor!

My love to you all.

Introduction

Brewing is a subjective undertaking. In some instances there is more than one way to brew a beer.

Many people have given me tidbits of brewing information which I have collected during the years as a homebrewer. The compilation of these tips, tricks, and techniques is what you will be getting in this book.

If you are a homebrewer with about 5–6 batches under your belt, you can learn about many different techniques and still be somewhat confused. After brewing 50–60 batches you will have reached a certain confidence level. But you still may want to learn about brewing gadgets and how to keep on brewing a truly great beer!

This book was written for all those brewers in mind. With this collection of tips from fellow homebrewers, homebrew shop owners, and professional brewers, you are getting the *best* of the best.

Some of the tips offered give you more than one way to accomplish the same thing. And depending upon your brewing level and the equipment you own, you may have to choose which is easiest for you at this point in time.

The goal of this book is to suggest alternative ways to your current brewing techniques—to make the brewing process easier and more fun.

Happy brewing!

David Weisberg
October 1995
Harrisville, New Hampshire

Table of Contents

Chapter One—
Brewing Basics

Chapter Two—
Improving
Homebrew Clarity

Chapter Three—
Keep It Clean

Chapter Four—
Yeast and Your Homebrew

Chapter Five—
Fermentation Made Simple

Chapter Six—
Hopping Like the Pros

Chapter Seven—
Bottling and Kegging Pointers

Chapter Eight—
Secrets from Fellow Homebrewers

Chapter Nine—
Traditional, All-Grain Brewing Demystified

Chapter Ten—
Homemade Brewing Gadgets

Acknowledgements

I want to thank the people who helped me with and/or encouraged me in the writing of this book.

Julie Weisberg, Margaret Gurney, Jim Fletcher, Barbara Bitzer-Richter, Jim Trautwein (*HomeBrewer's Software,* NC), Ray McNeill *(McNeill's Brewery,* VT), Frank Mengler, Jack Hayes, Matt Price, Dave Brown (*U-Brew Homebrew Supplies*, NH), Pamela & Carl Gammans (*NEPT*, NH).

Special thanks to the many homebrewers, friends, homebrew shop owners, and professional brewers who contributed their homebrewing ideas over the years.

Steve Cutter, Rick Faucher, Linda Fuerderer, Chris Heatley, Scott Moses, Randy Mosher, Kevin Sharp, *Adirondack Brewing Supply*, *Allen Biermakens*, Jim & Carol Whitely (*Arbor Wine & Beermaking Supplies Inc.*), David Ruggiero *(Barleymalt and Vine*, Newton MA), Matt (*Barleymalt and Vine*, Framingham MA), Glenn & Jacki-Ann Roy (*Beer Essentials*), Don Fisk (*Beer Makers of America Store & Pub*), James McHale (*Beer Unlimited*), Julian Bencomo (*Bencomo's Homebrew Supply*), Eric Marzewski (*Biermeister*), Charles Cowey (*Bonehead Brewing Co.*), Karl Menzer (*Bootleg Brew*), Miles D. Smith (*Brew America*), Wayne Cooke (*Brew Mart*), Reuben & Judi Rudd (*Brew Masters Ltd.*), Deborah Johnson (*Brew N' Kettle*), John Seckler (*Brewer, Cook, & Baker*), JD Adams & Tom Pfeffer (*Brewers Connection*), *Brother Logan Brewing Supplies*, Bev & Mike & Tracy Phillips (*Bucket of Suds*), Cliff Wyrick (*CJ's Beer & Wine Hobby Shop*), *Crossfire Home Brewing Supplies*, Scott Birdwell (*DeFalco's Home Wine & Beer Supplies*), *Doc's Cellar*, Edward Wren (*E.J. Wren Homebrew Inc.*), Peggi & Stephen Brose (*Easy Brewing*), *F.H. Steinbart Co.*, Dick & Karen Bemis *(Fermentation Settlement)*, Lee Knox (*Great Lakes Brew Supply*), Irene & Mark Shea (*Home Beer & Wine Supply, est. 1969*), Richard, Sr. & Richard, Jr. Leitz (*Home Brew Center*), Steve Norris (*Home Brew Co.*), Stephan Vernet (*Home Brewer's Outlet Inc.*), Jim & Bente Stockton (*Home Fermenter Center*), Douglas Faynor *(Homebrew Heaven*), Jon Scanlon (*Hops & Things*), Greg & Lynne Lawrence (*Lil' Olde*

Winemaking Shoppe), Brian Wood (*Lubbock Homebrew*), Mike Sebas & Mark Szamultulski (*Maltose Express*), Don Breton (*Maryland Homebrew*), Charles Culbreath & Michell Culhatt (*Mecca Coffee Co.*), Jim Dudley (*Mid-America Brewing*), Johnny Morrison (*Morrison's Homebrew*), Jacques & Ellen Patry *(Nashoba Brewing Supplies)*, Paul White (*Orfordville Home Brew Supplies*), Gloria & Bruce Franconi (*Party Creations*), Len Lemieux (*Pawtucket Homebrewing Supply*), Russell & Ellie Koontz (*Portable Potables*), James Waits (*The Beersmith*), John Fix III (*The Brew Shop at Cornell's*), David & Lisa Hoffmann (*The Brewmeister*), *The Brews Brothers at KEDCO*, Bob & Maryann (*The Flying Barrel*), *The Grape and Granary* (Akron, OH), Sam Wammack (*The Home Brewery*, MO), Frank & Robin Danesi (*The Home Brewery*, NV), Edward McDowell (*The Hop Shop Homebrew Supplies*), *The Purple Foot Downeast*, Alan Ebersold (*Third Fork Station*), Rhonda Berg (*The Whip & Spoon*), *U.S. Brewing Supply* (Albany NY), Daniel & Cynthia Soboti (*U-Brew*, NJ), Victor Trujillo (*Victor's Grape Arbor*), John Arthur (*What's Brewin'*), *Wheatsville Food CO-OP*, Dan Vega & Khalisa Kitz (*Whee Must Wort*), Ken, Scott, Steve, & Will (*WindRiver Brewing Co.*), John & Sheila Hubbard (*Wine and Beer Art of Smith Tompkins*), and Mark George (*Wine Barrel Plus*).

And special thanks to Betty Ann Sather for her help with the third edition.

Chapter One

Brewing Basics

Tip 1: Throw away the directions

When making beer from liquid malt extract kits, never follow the directions on the can. Why not? Most directions give you the easiest and quickest path toward brewing beer. Watery beer, but beer nonetheless. Instead follow these proven tips to help you brew the perfect pint.

— **Boil the wort**. If the wort (the sweet liquid soon to be homebrew; pronounced *wert*) is not boiled for at least 20 minutes, it cannot become sterilized and the hops will not completely do their job.

The longer you boil, the better hot-break you get. Hot-break occurs when protein trub (pronounced *troob*) coagulates during boiling and settles to the bottom of the brewpot. And hop oils are better able to dissolve with a one hour or longer boil.

> **Note:** With long boils your beer may become darker than you want. This is okay if that is what you are shooting for. If you are brewing a Pilsner style lager, you should boil for no more than one hour. If you are brewing a dark Bock beer, you should boil for at least 1–1½ hours.

— **Use malt extract instead of sugar.** When recipes call for corn sugar in the boil, try substituting dry malt extract. Sugar can lengthen fermentation time and sometimes causes off-flavors (i.e., cidery taste) in the final beer. Allow no more than 10% of the total weight of fermentables in your batch to be corn sugar. Even better, use no sugar at all (except maybe for carbonation).

— **Old dry yeast.** Yeast that comes with malt extract cans, if not kept in the refrigerator, can lose its viability within several months. To have a strong and clean fermentation—buy either fresh dry yeast or use liquid yeast (more on this in Chapter Four).

— **Two-stage fermentations**. Consider doing two-stage fermentations (i.e., using a 6.5-gallon plastic bucket for primary fermentation and a 5- or 6.5-gallon glass carboy for secondary fermentation). This allows for maximum beer clarity.

— **Add finishing hops.** Although most malt extract is hopped, you still should add aroma hops near (or at) the end of the boil to give you more hop flavor and aroma.

Tip 2: How to add malt extract to the brewpot without scorching

The best time to add dry malt extract is when the water in the brewpot is lukewarm, not boiling. Slowly add the extract while stirring. After the malt extract is dissolved, continue the boil.

Less mess: First pour dry malt extract (or corn sugar) into a clean container. Then pour from the container into the kettle. This avoids sticky messes with plastic bags—especially important when not using the whole bag.

When adding **malt extract syrup**, boil the water first. Then turn the heat completely off and add the malt. If using an electric stove, move the pot off the heating element before adding the syrup.

It is a good idea while waiting for the water to boil, to submerge the unopened malt can in hot water. This loosens the syrup and makes it easier to pour. Peel off any labels and stickers before opening the can.

Stir often until boiling begins. Whether brewing an extract or all-grain batch, keep the wort moving by stirring every few minutes or so until a full rolling boil starts. This technique keeps the malt from burning or caramelizing on the bottom of your brewpot.

Relax. Brewing is fun. Enjoy both brewing and drinking. – Russell Koontz, *Portable Potables*

Tip 3: Proper boiling speed and preventing boilovers

When boiling the wort, the first step to achieving the best burner level is to turn the burner (gas or electric) on high.

Once a fast rolling boil begins, turn the flame (or heat) down about 10%–15% (or just a hair). This keeps it rolling fast enough to allow the hop oils to dissolve and creates a good hot-break (protein coagulating and settling) without causing a boilover.

Electric brewers. Starting at the highest setting, turn down one notch from the highest as soon as a boil begins. This should keep your batch at a fast roll. If not, you will have to alternate every 5–10 minutes between highest setting and next-to-highest setting.

Lid ajar. It is best to keep the lid off the brewpot until a fast boil begins. This decreases your chances of a boilover (which can be a sticky mess to clean up).

Once boiling begins, prop the lid up a little. The best way to do this is by placing the long handle of a wooden spoon across the pot to keep the lid tilted up slightly. You should have about a one-inch gap through which the sweet smelling steam can escape.

Of course you still want to watch your brewpot from time to time. And NEVER leave the lid on without propping it up during the boil.

When the boil is finished put the lid completely on to prevent any contamination from getting into the wort.

Boilovers can be a REAL hot mess! One common sense tip is to use a brewpot large enough to accommodate a boilover. A 33-quart canning pot is great if you are boiling 5–6 gallons or less. You can quickly stop a boilover without losing too much of your wort.

— When a boilover occurs: Shut the flame (or heat) of your stove off immediately and carefully take the lid off. But do not try to move the brewpot!

A problem exists if you are using an electric stove. After you turn off an electric stovetop the heating element remains hot for a minute or so. It can be VERY dangerous trying to move a hot brewpot full of overflowing hot, sticky wort.

Two techniques to quickly stop a boilover:

— Throw in hops. Calm down the mad brew by throwing some loose whole hops into the brewpot. Watch out, if you throw in hop pellets it might make matters worse— sometimes pellets cause more foaming.

Either have a hop bag on hand with a few whole hops inside or have just a few loose whole hops handy to throw in to stop the mad, foaming-at-the-mouth boilover.

Murphy's Law of Brewing #45: The only time your wort boils over is when you leave the room or take your eyes off it.

—**Throw in cold water.** Have a small bowl filled with a pint of cold water ready to throw in the brewpot to calm things down. Adding ice cubes works too.

Tip 4: Control the brewing process

Using dark or amber malt extracts can cause some problems because you cannot always know exactly how they were formulated. For example, you might end up with a Porter overloaded with black malt astringency. And when using hopped malt extracts you rarely know the variety of hops and how much was used.

By **keeping control** of all the brewing ingredients you can brew any style of beer to any taste. Experiment and control the color and flavor by steeping specialty grains (i.e., caramel malt, black patent, roasted barley) below 170°F for 30 minutes and removing them prior to boil.

As a homebrewer you can put in the amount of bittering and finishing (aroma) hops you want. This involves YOU more in the brewing process, so a better homebrew results.

For an excellent quality Pilsner use all light dry malt extract, 3–5 different strains of fresh hops, no corn sugar (except maybe for priming), liquid yeast, and two-stage fermentation. Keep fermentation below 50°F (close to 40°F if possible). They might even have to call you a homebrew biermeister after this one! Save one for me.

Tip 5: Great racking tips

Racking is the process of transferring wort or beer from one container (i.e., brewpot, fermenter, or bottling bucket) into another container.

Prop it up. By placing a spare rubber stopper or a piece of 2 by 4 lumber under one side of your primary fermenter, you can cause the yeast sediment to settle in the far side. When racking from a plastic primary fermenter to a glass secondary fermenter, position the tip of your racking tube just above the sediment. Use a spring-loaded clothespin to hold the tube in place at the top of the primary fermenter. Now just siphon away.

With this simple trick you end up with more homebrew and less yeast sediment in your secondary fermenter.

Rack in the cold. If possible, use a spare refrigerator to cool down the wort when you are racking from the secondary to the bottling bucket. This technique will reduce oxidation in your homebrew. Try to gradually lower the temperature over a period of 2–3 days before racking. An ideal temperature to cool down to would be 40°–50°F. **Note:** Do not change the temperature more than 5°F per day— this could shock the yeast out of suspension.

Always bottle or prime with dry malt extract. It makes the difference.
— John Goode, *Wheatsville Food CO-OP*

Tip 6: Important recipe adjustments

When a recipe calls for liquid malt extract, but you want to use dry malt extract instead, simply multiply the given weight of liquid malt extract by 0.8 to get the correct amount of dry malt needed.

When a recipe calls for dry malt extract and you have only liquid malt extract, multiple the weight of dry malt by 1.25 to get the correct amount of liquid malt extract needed. Adjust your recipes accordingly in your brew log (see Tip 7).

Hopping adjustments:

— If you are in a habit of using **muslin hop bags** to hold your hops during the boil, then add 10–15% more hops to keep the correct bitterness and/or aroma levels.

It is harder for bitterness/aroma to be extracted when hops are in a bag since there is less surface area making contact with the wort.

— When doing a **partial-wort boil** (i.e., 3 gallons boiled, then 2½ gallons of water added)—add 30-50% more hops. You will get much less hop bitterness from the same amount of hops with highly concentrated worts. So hop *much* more when doing partial-wort boils!

Tip 7: Record keeping—your brew log

You will find it **very important to keep accurate records** of your brewing efforts. The following are just some of the items to include in your brew log: temperature, ingredients, specific gravity, hop strain, amount of hops, yeast strain, batch number, batch name, and brewing/tasting notes.

It is a good idea to **use down-time** during a brew session to fill out your brew log. Then throughout the fermentation and conditioning stages, record temperature and gravities.

Three-ring binders work great for holding your brew log sheets (hole-punched). *See brew log sample below.*

Computerized brew logging. The latest trend for homebrewers with computers is to use one of several brewing/logging software packages. They enable you to use or alter existing recipes from a database or to create your own. In some cases, you can create your own labels and calculate bittering and alcohol levels. Some of the better packages offer a very elaborate training section.

Take good notes. There is nothing worse than having a homebrew that turns out to be fantastic and not being able to remember what was in it or how you did it. But damn, it was good.
— Charles Cowey, *Bonehead Brewing Co.*

DATE:	STYLE:	BATCH#:
NAME:		BREWER(S):

Recipe   HOMEBREW LOG

QTY	UNIT	INGREDIENTS
=====	=====	===
_____	_____	_____
_____	_____	_____
_____	_____	_____
_____	_____	_____
_____	_____	_____
_____	_____	_____
_____	_____	_____
_____	_____	_____
_____	_____	_____
_____	_____	_____
_____	_____	_____
_____	_____	_____
_____	_____	_____
_____	_____	_____

Hopping Schedule

BOIL TIME	HOP VARIETY	OUNCES	ALPHA%	AAU TOT	Factor	IBU TOT
=========	====================	======	======	=======	======	=======
_____	_____	____	____	_____	____	_____
_____	_____	____	____	_____	____	_____
_____	_____	____	____	_____	____	_____
_____	_____	____	____	_____	____	_____
_____	_____	____	____	_____	____	_____

BOIL:_____ mins. Dry hopping?:_____   TOTAL IBUs: _____

Fermentation/Conditioning

	Start Date	Finish Date	# of days	Ave Temp (F)	Specific Gravity
Primary	_____	_____	_____	_____	O.G.: _____
Secondary	_____	_____	_____	_____	T.G.: _____
Conditioning	_____	_____	_____	_____	Alc%: _____

[ ]-bottled   [ ]-kegged   Priming Type/Amt.?:_____

(Brewing notes and tasting notes on reverse)

Sample brew log. Keep good notes--make good beer.

Chapter Two

Improving Homebrew Clarity

Tip 8: Partial-wort boil chilling technique

Instead of doing a full-wort boil (i.e., boiling 5–6 gallons of wort) you can boil just 2 gallons. Before you start your brew session, pour 4 gallons of pre-boiled or spring water into four 1-gallon plastic water jugs and stick them in the freezer. Check jugs once an hour to make sure they do not freeze. When your brew is 5 minutes away from the end of boil, take out the water. Pour 3 gallons of the 'starting-to-freeze' water into your cleaned and sanitized fermenter.

As soon as you turn the heat off take a small sanitized saucepan and gently ladle the wort through a sanitized, screened colander into a large funnel positioned above the fermenter.

> **Caution:** Do not attempt to pour the entire contents in at once. Scalding hot wort can burn on contact!

If using a glass carboy, always add the cold water before adding the hot wort. This way the cold water can buffer the glass from thermal shock. As the hot wort hits the cold water, the temperature drops almost instantly. After all the wort has been ladled into the fermenter, check the liquid level. If necessary top up the fermenter with cold water from the fourth gallon until you reach the correct level (i.e., 5–5½ gallons).

Take a temperature reading. Wait until the temperature drops below 75-80°F before pitching ale yeast, and below 50-55°F before pitching lager yeast. If you do not wait until the wort temperature is correct, you may kill the yeast (i.e., at 120°F or greater).

Tip 9: Three ways to quickly cool wort temperature

Immersion wort chiller. This device—used when the boiling process is done—quickly cools wort to the proper temperature. Cold water runs through a long coiled copper pipe which is immersed in the brewpot. To kill bacteria on the chiller place it in the brewpot 15 minutes before the end of boil.

The immersion wort chiller is easy to clean and is virtually bug-free because malt touches only the outside of the tubing (not the inside). It cools 3 gallons of wort down to yeast pitching temperature in 15–20 minutes.

Counter-flow type wort chiller. This chiller runs hot wort through one pipe (usually a copper inner pipe) and cold water in the other direction through an outer pipe or container. It can be both difficult and time consuming to clean out the inside of a counter-flow wort chiller before and after running wort through it. If you have a pump you can quickly run sanitizer through it. However since pumps can cost $80–$120, the immersion wort chiller is preferred by most homebrewers.

The following tip saves water if you either have to conserve during water shortages, or if you have a well and cannot always let water run for 15–20 minutes as needed with wort chillers.

Frozen plastic soda bottles. Take two or more empty 2-liter soda bottles, clean off labels and any glue, fill with water (75% full), recap, and freeze. When you are ready to chill your wort, remove the bottles from the freezer, place them in a no-rinse sanitizer for at least 5 minutes, and shake dry. Put them in the brewpot and you will have a quickly chilled wort. After about five minutes you may want to remove the first set, and add other frozen ones.

Never attempt to brew Zima.
                              — Miles D. Smith, *Brew America*

Tip 10: Brew crystal-clear beers

If you want a really clear beer, here are four methods you can use.

1. Irish Moss. Adding one teaspoon of Irish Moss (basically dried red marine algae) 5–30 minutes before the end of the boil helps settle out proteins which can cause haze in your homebrew.

2. Unsweetened gelatin added to the secondary fermenter 8–10 days before bottling also clears your beer (works best on lagers).

To use gelatin—add one pint of cold water to a small saucepan. Add 1½ teaspoons of gelatin per 5-gallon batch. After it is dissolved in the water, turn the heat on low and stir from time to time. Just *before* it reaches a boil shut the heat off instantly. Remove the gelatin solution from the burner if using an electric stove.

> **Note:** Boiling this solution causes the gelatin to gel. Do not boil unless you want *jello*^{TM}*-beer*.

Gently add the solution to the bottom of the empty secondary fermenter. Transfer the wort on top of it to mix the gelatin into the wort. To increase the efficiency of the gelatin slowly (over 2–3 days) bring the temperature of the secondary down to 50°F or lower—the closer to freezing the better. Wait at least 8–10 days and then bottle.

3. *Chill* your *homey* for 2 days in a spare refrigerator before you bottle. Aim for 40°–50°F. This allows more protein trub, hops, and yeast to settle to the bottom of the secondary— which stays behind when you bottle or keg.

An old fridge and a new temp. controller do the trick!

4. A water filter can be used when kegging your beer and carbonating with CO_2 (not priming solution). Use a soda keg as a secondary fermenter and transfer through the filter into a serving keg. By using different size filters you can either get rid of just the yeast or create a brilliantly clear brew.

Filtering overview: After everything has been sanitized you need to purge any O_2 with CO_2 from the system (this is important to keep beer fresh and unoxidized). Fill the serving keg with CO_2. Then, with the CO_2 tank set at 20 psi, connect everything as follows: Liquid-out from the fermenter/keg connected to filter-in side of the filter. Connect the filter-out line to the liquid-out connector on the serving keg. Leave the serving keg's lid ajar while filtering the beer. Now the beer will flow through the filter into the serving keg. Carbonate keg as usual. Done!

One way to create micro-brewery quality beer at home.

Filter compliments of The Filter Store.

Chapter Three

Keep It Clean

Tip 11: Cleanliness is next to godliness

S anitation is easy with one tablespoon of household bleach to five gallons of water. Soak every surface, utensil, instrument, or container in this solution for 20–30 minutes. Then (while wearing rubber gloves) rinse everything thoroughly with hot tap water to rinse any chlorine residue.

Or instead of rinsing—shake and let dry for several hours.

Iodine-based sanitizers are best because no rinsing is required. They are widely used in the pub/micro industry.   – Jim Dudley, *Mid-America Brewing Co.*

— **Filter chlorinated water.** Or preboil and let cool overnight.

— **Clean those soda kegs (cornelius canister).** If your soda kegs get a hard, brown stain on the bottom, use B-Brite™ (a cleanser) and hot water. Fill soda keg ⅓-full with a B-Brite™ solution, let soak for 2 hours, and scrub with a NEW toilet brush (don't be a skinflint and use an old brush!). Rinse well.

—**Turbo carboy rinsing.** To speed up emptying your carboy of sanitizing solution, take the plastic tip off your rigid racking tube or cane. Insert the tube through the neck and into the bottom of the carboy. As you tilt the carboy toward your sink, hold the tube so one end is in the airspace and the other end is coming out of the neck.

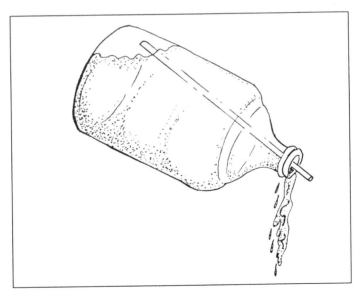

Rinse carboys twice as fast with this simple trick!

Because no vacuum is present the carboy empties VERY quickly. Works great!

— **Picnic spigots** (cobra head dispensers) and most other beer taps come apart fairly easily for cleaning. Be sure to clean them between usage. They really get gunked up and can affect the taste of your draft beer.

— **Cleaning out beer kegs** (i.e., 7.75-, 15.5-gallon size with a small opening). Use an auto mechanic's inspection mirror and flashlight to see how clean you got your keg—or how clean you STILL need to get it.

— **Jet spray.** One of the best bottle and carboy washers around is the jet-style bottle washer. Made of brass, it attaches to your sink faucet with a garden hose faucet adapter. It sprays a powerful jet of water into your bottles or carboys and makes for quick cleanup.

Attach a garden hose 'Y' connector on your faucet so you can leave the bottle washer on one of the outlets permanently. The other outlet can be used for rinsing.

Be careful to only press the water release lever of the bottle washer when a bottle is on the jet or you might end up with a very wet, but clean, ceiling (or face).

I have successfully avoided dealing with chemical sanitizers by keeping bottles and equipment "physically" clean by brushing, wiping, etc., and by thoroughly rinsing everything with scalding tap water.
– Dan Vega, *Whee Must Wort Homebrewing Supplies*

Tip 12: Tired of washing those dirty bottles?

This great bottling tip solves part of the drudgery of bottle washing and saves you time (leaving you with more time for drinking your creations).

Before filling the bottles clean them with hot water and inspect the insides. Then place all your bottles in a cold oven and heat to 200°F for 10 minutes. No fussing and no scrubbing. And no mess. Your bottles are quickly sanitized. Just be sure NOT to touch the tops or insides of the bottles while you are removing them— otherwise you might introduce bacteria.

Avoid using this technique when bottling with Grolsch™ type swing-top bottles. The rubber gaskets or the plastic tops (found on some) could melt into a gooey mess! *Holy melted mess Batman!*

When using swing-top bottles, just sanitize using scalding hot water (or weak bleach solution) and let dry.

After finishing a bottle of beer, clean your bottle right away to avoid letting your brew stick to the inside of the bottle.
— Richard C. Leitz, Sr. & Leitz, Jr., *Home Brew Center*

Tip 13: Clean and simple ways to start a siphon

Whenever you need to move wort (or beer) from one container to another do not use your mouth to start the siphon. Too much bacteria lives in your mouth (even after gargling with vodka or brandy).

Instead try the following simple methods:

Water siphon. After cleaning and sanitizing your siphon tube hold both open ends upward at an even elevation. Now fill the tube with water.

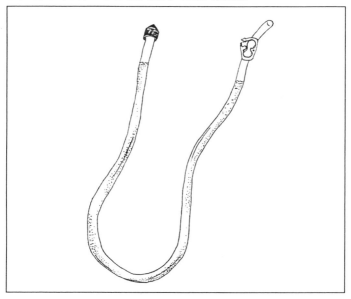

Racking tube and hose filled with water.

Next, clip a plastic siphon hose clamp tightly (in the closed position) on the outflow end of the tube. Place the inflow end (the end with the siphon tip) into your full fermenter. Now lower the outflow end with the clamp toward a small bucket. Open the clamp.

First water flows out, then your beer. Spill the water into the bucket, then clamp the siphon shut again. Move the tube to the receiving container and let the homebrew flow.

Minimize splashing. Remember not to splash your homebrew when racking. If you do splash, you may end up with an oxidized beer with little or no hop bouquet.

Turkey baster. Use a turkey baster to easily start a siphon. Buy a separate one for this purpose— do not try using your kitchen one (yucch!).

You may need to use a small piece of duct tape around the baster where the ball-end goes over the basting tube. This gives you better vacuum power by not letting air leak in.

After sanitizing your rigid racking tube, flexible racking hose, and baster, insert the tip of the baster tightly into the output end of your racking hose. Squeeze the baster ball tight, then place the inflow end of the racking tube into your beer.

Now let go of the baster ball. As the liquid starts to flow towards the baster quickly pull the baster out and let the liquid flow.

Or instead of pulling the baster out in mid-flow (which can be messy) use a siphon hose clamp and close it as soon as the siphon hose is full of liquid. Remove the baster then open the clamp to start the flow again.

Take hydrometer reading samples with a baster. Squeeze the ball end, lower the baster (with rigid racking tube or racking cane attached) into the wort, and release the ball end. Pull the tube out of the wort and squeeze your sample into the sample tube. Two samplings should give you enough wort for a hydrometer reading. If not, repeat. Clean, simple, and quick!

When taking hydrometer samples from your fermenter, take the racking tube tip off and sample from the center of the wort. Taking the tip off allows you to easily fill the sample holder. Sampling from the center gives you an accurate sample with the least amount of yeast and trub.

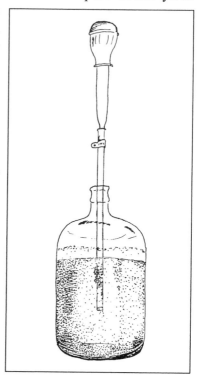

Turkey baster and racking tube. Two squeezes for a clean sample.

Keep the lid open during a boil with a handy clothespin.

It's easy to be an environmental brewer. Remove the tops and bottoms on empty malt extract cans, crush flat, and add to your recycling. And go easy on bleach and iodine—a little of these nasty chemicals goes a long way!

Chapter Four

Yeast and Your Homebrew

Tip 14: Care and feeding of yeast beasties

Strengthen dry yeast power with a simple process called rehydration. Boil one cup of water for 10–15 minutes and cool (covered) to 100°–105°F. Pour water into a sanitized one-quart measuring pitcher and empty the dry yeast into the water. Cover with sanitized aluminum foil and let stand for 10 minutes. Do not let it stand for more than 20 minutes.

Bring the temperature down to the wort's temperature by placing it in your refrigerator. Now add this yeast and water solution to the cooled wort.

— **Dry lager yeast?** When using a dry lager yeast, you never get true lager yeast. To brew a true lager style beer you MUST use liquid yeast.

— **Aeration of the wort is absolutely necessary.** If you are using a plastic bucket for fermentation, use a sanitized metal whisk reserved just for brewing to aerate your wort prior to adding the yeast. Try not to bump and scratch the sides of the bucket with the whisk because scratches can harbor bacteria. To keep things clean wear a rubber glove when whisking.

If you are using a glass fermenter, rock the carboy back and forth for several minutes every hour until fermentation begins (i.e., showing signs of CO_2 production). Limit the wort's amount of exposure to oxygen once fermentation begins otherwise your final brew may have off-flavors.

— **Yeast starter alive and kicking.** A yeast starter is a small amount of wort used to increase the yeast population 12–48 hours prior to brewing. With a large enough active yeast population you will get a fast and healthy fermentation. About 4–6 ounces of yeast slurry is recommended for pitching a 5-gallon batch.

I boil all my beers hard . . . for 90 minutes. Full-boil!
– Ray McNeill, *McNeill's Brewery* (Brattleboro, VT.)
(Editor's note: regarding all-grain brewing)

Tip 15: Save money on liquid yeast by re-using it from batch to batch

Because liquid yeast is 2–3 times more expensive than regular dry yeast, this tip will save you money.

Buy one package of liquid yeast for a batch and brew as you normally do. When transferring from the primary fermenter to the secondary fermenter, leave roughly one cup of wort behind in the bottom of the fermenter (*no, you are not going to drink it*).

Swirl the yeast and the remaining wort in the bottom of the fermenter to loosen up the yeast. While wearing sanitized rubber gloves, take a paper towel dipped in a high alcohol liquor (i.e., vodka) and wipe the inside of the neck and top area of the carboy (or the plastic primary fermenter).

Next clean and sanitize a small funnel, a large champagne bottle (or one-quart canning jar), and a small piece of aluminum foil. Now pour 1–2 pints of the mixed yeast slurry through the funnel into the champagne bottle or canning jar. Avoid breathing on the yeast during these procedures to prevent possible contamination. Wrap the piece of aluminum foil over the top of the bottle and put the bottle in the back of your refrigerator.

You now have just saved high quality yeast ready for the next batch. It is best to use the yeast within 3–5 days. When saving yeast from a previous batch it is important to use hop bags for your hops, otherwise you may get pieces of hops mixed in with the yeast.

Avoid using this yeast-saving method with any batch to which you add specialty items (i.e., chili peppers, spices, berries, wood chips). Otherwise the same flavor may end up in all the batches you use this yeast with.

When you are ready to re-use the yeast prepare a yeast starter by boiling 4–5 cups of water with one cup of dry malt extract and 2–3 hop pellets for 15–20 minutes. Let the starter cool to 68°–73°F, and then funnel it into another champagne bottle or mason jar. Use a paper towel dipped in vodka or all-grain alcohol (*not* rubbing alcohol) to sanitize the inside mouth of the champagne bottle or canning jar containing the yeast.

Pour off the top layer of wort from the previous batch then swirl around the yeast to loosen it from the bottom. Now add the yeast to the cooled yeast starter using a sanitized funnel, and aerate. The starter should be ready for pitching within 6–18 hours.

> **Caution:** When saving yeast in your refrigerator never have the bottle or jar tightly capped! Check it daily and release any CO_2 build-up which may have occurred. A lot of CO_2 pressure can be generated so make sure it can get out. This avoids any possibilities of a yeast bottle or jar exploding in your refrigerator and totally ruining your day.

An even easier yeast re-using technique is to pitch the yeast from the bottom of one primary (ready to be racked into a secondary) into a new batch (just boiled and cooled). This will keep the yeast clean and very powerful. Your lag time might only be a few hours when repitching with this method. Of course you would need to time your brew sessions closer together—but this means more beer!

Tip 16: Using liquid yeast cultures like the pros

L iquid yeast is the purest yeast you can buy. By using it properly you can make professional tasting homebrew every time you brew.

STEP 1: Keep your yeast refrigerated until you are ready to use it. When ready, remove the packet from the fridge and let it warm to room temperature. Place the packet on a hard surface and pop the bulge. Now wait till it swells to about one-inch thick.

> **Note:** For every month after the date stamped on the package it takes approximately one day extra for the yeast package to swell.

STEP 2: Make a starter culture. You must do this because there just simply is not enough yeast to start a proper fermentation. You should pitch 16–32 ounces of starter culture per 5 gallons of beer. (You should have 4–6 ounces of yeast slurry/sediment from the 16–32 ounces starter culture.)

To make a starter culture boil 4–5 cups of water with one cup of dried malt extract for 15 minutes. If you like, add a few hop pellets to create a somewhat acidic solution. Bacteria will not survive in an acidic solution. Cool the solution to 68°–73°F.

> **Note:** The color of the malt extract (e.g., light, amber, or dark) you use in the starter should match the beer you are creating.

STEP 3: Pour the starter wort into a 40-ounce sanitized bottle leaving several inches of space between the bulb and neck of the bottle. Sanitize the packet of yeast, cut it open, and pour it into the starter wort. Affix an airlock to the bottle and keep it in a dark place overnight till you are ready to pitch. A champagne bottle with a #1 rubber stopper and airlock works well.

STEP 4: PITCHING: When ready to pitch yeast remove the airlock and wipe the mouth of the bottle with sanitizing solution. Swirl the starter to resuspend the yeast and pitch immediately.

> **Note:** Avoid breathing on the yeast during this process because the wide variety of bacteria on your breath would live all too happily in the yeast solution.

STEP 5: Aerate the wort by stirring (or shaking) vigorously for a minute, then close the fermenter. Fermentation should begin in 6–18 hours—the sooner the better.

[Source: David & Lisa Hoffmann, *The Brewmeister* homebrew shop]

By using a yeast starter you will have a much shorter lag time between the time you pitch the yeast and when it begins showing signs of fermentation. Your wort will be less susceptible to infections and you will greatly improve the quality of your homebrew.

2-quart juice jars are great for holding yeast starters.

Always, always, always agitate/stir vigorously when adding yeast. Yeast needs oxygen to live also.
   – Don Breton, *Maryland Homebrew*

**JoJo's famous homebrew--contains all natural
ingredients!**

*Liquid yeast cultures are worth the time. Without
yeast, all other ingredients don't mean much. With
some time and planning, the homebrewer will pro-
duce fantastic brews.*

— The Brews Brothers at KEDCO

Chapter Five

Fermentation Made Simple

Tip 17: Fermentation basics

Mark the sides of your fermenters. When using a plastic primary fermenter it is helpful to mark the sides with a permanent marking pen in 1-gallon increments. With glass fermenters you can mark the sides with a dark color nail polish.

This saves you time when adding hot wort and topping off the fermenter with cold water. Now you can quickly fill to the correct level without taking time to carefully measure each pour.

— **Plastic or glass?** Avoid using plastic buckets for longer than 4–5 days because it is very likely oxygen will find its way into your beer and cause problems. Once CO_2 production slows down in the primary fermenter the outward pressure on the walls of a plastic bucket decreases. Since the plastic used in plastic buckets is oxygen permeable, oxygen will slowly leak into your fermenter and into your homebrew, robbing hop bouquet.

Plastic is okay for primary fermentations. But once the foam head falls it is much better to transfer the wort into a glass carboy for your secondary fermentations.

—Control temperature. You must try controlling the temperature in and around your precious fermenting brew. Unless you have a basement with a separate cold box and/or root cellar, you need to be resourceful (as most homebrewers are). Several of the following tips can be used to control temperature:

1. Use styrofoam (which some glass carboys are shipped in) to wrap around the carboy.

> **Note:** Do not put the styrofoam jacket on until the wort temperature has dropped to the desired fermentation level. Otherwise, the jacket could keep the temperature too high during the first 12–24 hours.

2. Bulkhead door. If you live in a cold climate and have an outside bulkhead door with stairs leading down to your basement—position your fermenter near the lower door (inside your basement). Open and close the lower door as needed to control the temperature during the cold months.

3. Spare refrigerator. If you live in a warm climate (or during the summer) you can use a **spare refrigerator** with a special temperature control device (i.e., controls temperature between 32°–80°F; unit costs between $30-$100). Make sure you do not keep food in the same fridge, because temperatures for fermenting beer might not be too great for last night's tuna casserole!

4. Insulate. If your fermentation area is too cold, use some type of rigid or batt insulation to wrap around your fermenter. Newer house insulation comes wrapped in plastic so people do not get the itchies during installation (and you can use it so your homebrew does not get the itchies either).

— Check the specific gravity. Specific gravity gives you a reading of how dense your wort is compared with water (e.g., 1.000 degrees specific gravity for water). Original Gravity tells you how much sugar is present (and potential alcohol level can be estimated) before the yeast is pitched. Final Gravity tells you how much sugar is left after fermentation is complete.

Knowing the specific gravity before, during, and after fermentation allows you to better track fermentation and calculate the alcohol level of your final homebrew.

— Wild fermentations! If you find foam in your airlock—clean and sanitize the airlock immediately. When your airlock is full of foam, and there is a continuous liquid path from the outside air into your wort—you are just asking for problems with contamination.

Either the level of the wort was too close to the top of the fermenter or the fermentation temperature was too high. In either case try moving the fermenter to a cooler location. If you still have foaming problems, remove the airlock and install a blow-off tube running into a small bucket filled with a weak sanitizing solution.

Tip 18: Use a blow-off tube during first two days of fermentation

This technique is especially useful when brewing a light lager because some of the harsh hop resins are blown out the tube. You will have a smoother, cleaner tasting beer for all your efforts.

A **blow-off tube** can be made by inserting a 3-foot length of $3/4$"–1" dia. food-grade plastic tubing into the neck of a glass carboy (primary fermenter). Place the other end of the tube into a 2-quart glass jug half filled with weak sanitizing solution.

Some of the rocky krausen head (thick layer of foam in the primary) during fermentation may foam out into the jar. Assume you will lose 1–2 quarts of your beer. Clean the jar out daily. In 2–3 days (or after the foaming stops) replace the tube with a regular airlock.

Always take your starting gravity and WRITE IT DOWN and keep taking readings.
– Jim Whitely, *Arbor Wine & Beermaking Supplies, Inc.*

Tip 19: Lifting and moving wort and beer

Since you are most likely to be brewing in 5-gallon batch sizes, the most you have to lift is 40–50 pounds. Here are a few ways to save your back and to avoid brewing disasters.

— **Milk crates** can be found kicking around in every-one's basement, closet, or garage. These square plastic jobbers are *great*. They come with handles and most glass carboys and plastic fermenters fit in just fine. You might have to wrap a towel around the base of a carboy or a plastic fermenter to make a tighter fit.

Three Amigos--toweled, crated, ready for action.

— **A carboy handle** on the neck of a carboy is another way to *get a grip*. However, do NOT use the handle to lift the whole weight of the carboy—the neck is *not* strong enough for this. Instead use the handle to tilt the carboy enough to get your hands under it. Then lift with your hands under the bottom of the carboy. *Remember to bend those knees!*

— **Pump it, don't lift it.** One advanced tip is to use an electric pump (usually $80–$120) specifically designed to move hot liquids. This is similar to the way commercial breweries do it. You do not see commercial breweries trying to move giant fermenters around! Instead they pump the beer.

By using a pump you can keep your fermenters (primary and secondary) in place at any height. For example, both primary and secondary fermenters can be on the same shelf— right next to each other. And the kettle can be on the same level too. By using a pump (which needs to be sanitized before and after use) you can pump wort from the kettle to the primary. And then 5–7 days (depending on fermentation) later, pump wort from the primary fermenter to the secondary fermenter.

It is recommended to use pumps when brewing in 15-gallon or larger batches. Otherwise it takes too much time waiting for gravity or a siphon to move the liquid. The logistics of moving that much homebrew can be unwieldy. So pump it.

One disadvantage of pumps is they may introduce unwanted aeration (depending on the quality of the pump you buy). Aeration is necessary for fermentation of the wort *only* when you are pitching yeast. When the wort is still hot or fermentation has already begun, you should NEVER aerate it. Oxygenation (or aeration) at these stages rob hop bouquet and create a stale taste in the final beer.

Always be careful when using electricity next to any water. A GFIC (ground fault interrupt circuit) electrical outlet is always recommended for any electrical device being used close to sink areas. Hire a licensed electrician to install a GFIC.

Tip 20: Triple your lagering space by fermenting in soda kegs

The best material for a fermenter is stainless steel. But most homebrewers ferment in glass or plastic.

Plastic is lightweight and durable, but if scratches develop inside from cleaning and use, bacteria can get a stronghold. Plus, during long fermentations oxygen can creep in through the plastic walls of a plastic bucket.

Glass is great. Except do not drop it (crash!). Watch out for thermal shock too. An extreme change from hot to cold, or cold to hot, can crack and/or break the glass.

Stainless steel however is durable, easy to clean, and resistant to thermal shock. It is everything except cheap (when buying new)—but worth it.

If you have your glass secondary fermenter in a spare refrigerator, you might only have room for one fermenter. However, if you have several soda kegs handy, follow these steps to make room for more lagering homebrew.

Soda keg used as a secondary fermenter.

1. Transfer to the keg. When it is time to transfer from primary to secondary—instead of transferring to a glass carboy—transfer to a cleaned and sanitized stainless steel 5-gallon soda keg. Watch inside the keg as the liquid level rises to the top. Make sure you fill to no more than one inch below the gas-in tube (inside the keg). If the liquid level rises above the bottom of this tube, the CO_2 being produced cannot be released from the keg!

2. Close the lid and seal with 10 psi of CO_2. Then, to create an airlock, connect a 3-foot length plastic tube to the gas-in connector using a metal tube clamp. Run the other end of the tube into a $1/2$-gallon jug half filled with a weak sanitizing solution.

3. Place the soda keg and the jug in your spare refrigerator (with all the racks taken out). Put the open end of the tube into the water jug and—while holding the tube in place—attach the gas-in connector to the keg. At this point a lot of CO_2 will be released so hold the tube underwater until it stops jumping around.

You now have an airlock for your fermenter!

It is simple to add 2–3 other fermenters using the above steps. You may have to fashion a clip to hold the ends of the tubes in place underwater. When moving kegs in and out of the fridge, remove the connectors so homebrew does not accidentally spill out through the airlock tube.

Don't let bottling get you down. Move to kegging to make your brewing a more pleasurable experience.
    – Eric Marzewski, *Biermeister*

Tip 21: Increase your brew size by fermenting in beer kegs

Ever considered using 7.75- or 15.5- gallon kegs (also called ¼- and ½-barrels) as fermenters? You can probably buy a used keg from a beer distributor for $25–$35. Or look around at metal recycling businesses for one. Before buying be sure to carefully inspect kegs for cracks and holes.

By removing the ball-lock/stem assembly from a typical keg, and using a #10.5 drilled rubber stopper, you can ferment in the keg! Remove the pressure first by tapping any remaining beer with the correct tap connector. If the keg is empty, push down on the valve and slowly release pressure.

> **Caution:** It can be tricky (and sometimes dangerous) removing the ball-lock/stem assembly from the keg. Consider purchasing a special tool to remove the stem. One tool currently available is called *KegMan* produced by *Crossfire HomeBrewing Supplies* (203-623-6537).

Brew a 5-gallon batch and transfer the wort into a 7.75-gallon keg to be used as a primary fermenter. Then top up with preboiled (and cooled) water to the correct level. Leave enough room for foaming during fermentation. Or fill 2–3 inches from the top if you are using the blow-off fermentation method.

> **Note:** Add enough malt into the brewpot for a 7½-gallon batch, or else the beer will be weak.

Brewing a 15-gallon batch. Use two 15.5-gallon kegs (one for primary and one for secondary). When secondary fermentation is done, transfer your beer into the empty primary fermenter which now becomes your dispensing keg.

Yeast sediment. If you are worried about yeast sediment in your keg, remove the inside dip-tube stem and cut ½–¾ inch off the end using a hacksaw. The dip-tube stem normally rests slightly off the bottom of the keg to get as much of the beer out of the keg as possible. After you shorten the stem it will rest just above the yeast sediment. You will get clear beer from the first pull!

Bad back warning. Unless your first name is *Arnold*, do not plan on moving a full 15.5-gallon fermenter by yourself. You need an easy way to transfer into and out of this large vessel. If you are not using an electric pump, position the fermenter(s) for the best use of gravity before filling them.

> *Use glass fermenters, both for primary and secondary.*
> — David Ruggiero, *Barleymalt and Vine*

When using a small-mouthed carboy, put the airlock in the stopper *before* your put the stopper in the carboy—or you could end up with a very small ship in a very big bottle.—*Rick Bestany*

Try using a large, metal tea ball (as found in restaurant supply stores) to hold hops when dry hopping. The weight of the stainless-steel sinks the hops down into the bottom of a soda keg—makes dry hopping easy!
Source: John Farver (*Fermentation Noise*, Yakima, WA)

There is a device originally intended for opening sheet rock compound or driveway sealing compounds buckets found at most hardware stores. It makes a great tool for opening your primary plastic fermenter. I purchased mine for 79 cents in 1994.
—*Byron Bromley*

Please don't be in a terrible rush to bottle. Allow the beer to finish completely, settle a little to help clarify, then bottle.
  – Douglas Faynor, *Homebrew Heaven*

Chapter Six

Hopping Like the Pros

Tip 22: The road to delicious, hoppy homebrew

The first step toward easy and deliciously hoppy beers is to avoid heavy use of high alpha acid hops. These can be strong and overpowering. Instead use more hops with lower alpha acids ratings (aroma hops) to get a really flavorful and aromatic homebrew. Alpha acid levels can range from 2%–13% (low:2–4%, medium:5%–7%, high:8%–13%).

For example, try to limit your use of hops with greater than 8% alpha acid ratings. High alpha acid hop strains are used more often in stouts and higher-alcohol beers.

Hopping for flavor and aroma: Using a low-to-medium alpha acid hop, add $\frac{1}{2}$–1 ounce 20 minutes before end of boil and 1–2 ounces at the end of boil. This will give your beer amazing hop flavor and hop bouquet.

The 1–2 ounce level at the end of the boil is designed strictly for the hop-heads among us. Give it a try at these levels. Then adjust the hopping if your taste buds get assaulted, or your wallet gets thinner (hops can be expensive if you are buying them fresh).

Of course hopping depends on the hop level you need. And this depends on style and how much malt you have in your brew. A balanced beer has the right amount of hops for the right amount of malt, i.e., not too much malty sweetness and not overly bitter.

Easy hopping. When hopping during boiling at different times (i.e., 60, 20, and zero minutes before end of boil), use a separate hop/muslin bag for each hopping. This technique makes for easy clean-up and you do not have to strain the wort into the fermenter.

When using compressed hop plugs make sure you allow enough room for expansion—do not overfill the hop bags. When hop plugs get soaked, they will expand.

If you want a great hop aroma, try this simple technique: On the second day of fermentation, throw about 5-10 pellets in the primary.
          – Karl Menzer, Bootleg Brew

Tip 23: Large-scale brewing techniques for homebrewers

Some microbreweries pump their wort from the kettle (brewpot) into an area (grant) containing fresh hops, before sending the wort to be chilled down to yeast pitching temperature.

— Siphon wort over fresh hops. Siphon the hot (but not boiling) wort from the brewpot over a muslin hop bag containing 1–1½ ounces of aroma hops (i.e., less than 5%–6 % alpha acid rating).

By placing the hop bag in a colander (resting in a large funnel) you will prevent the bag from clogging the funnel.

Notice colander in funnel. Mengler (L), Weisberg (R)

By siphoning hot wort over the hops you reduce the chance of infection from the unsterilized hops. And you will get professional-quality hop bouquet in your final brew!

Note: When siphoning hot liquid use a 16"–20" copper racking cane attached to your siphon hose to absorb the heat.

— **Variety is the spice of life.** The more varieties of hops you use, the better. Besides creating complexity, different varieties can mask the off-flavors of one individual strain.

Large breweries always aim for a consistent and clean beer to sell. Some mega-breweries are known to use as many as 8–10 different hop strains in a given batch!

For you (the homebrewer) 3–5 different hop strains would be enough. Give it a try with hop pellets. Buy one-ounce packets of 3–5 different hop strains. Then use several different strains together at different times throughout the boil (i.e., 60, 45, 30, 10, and 2 minutes before the end of the boil).

Tip 24: Dry hopping for success

Dry hopping is the traditional British brewing technique of adding hops into a secondary fermenter, or cask, to get a great hop bouquet (also called hop nose).

— **What is the best way to dry hop?** If you use stainless steel soda kegs for secondary fermentation try the following trick.

When racking the wort from the primary fermenter into the secondary (soda keg) fermenter, add $\frac{1}{4}$–$\frac{1}{2}$ ounce of a nice aroma whole hops (e.g., Saaz, Cascade) into a sanitized hop bag. Before tying the bag closed, add 15–20 large sanitized marbles. Close the bag and wrap the draw string around the bag's neck a few times. Now toss the bag into the soda keg fermenter and gently rack your homebrew onto it.

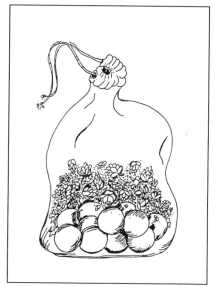

Sanitized marbles sink hop bag to bottom of soda keg.

The longer you leave the secondary alone (*and it is hard to wait, isn't it?*) the better your hop bouquet will be. Let those hops mingle with your homebrew for 1–2 weeks.

> **Note:** When racking from the soda keg into a bottling bucket make sure the hop bag does not get in the way of the racking tube.

When dry hopping use either whole flower hops, pellets, or hop plugs to create a superb hop aroma. Keep in mind that hop pellets tend to cause the least trouble (clogging) when siphoning.

— **Fresh hops only**. Dry hopping is a waste of time if you are using old or stale hops. Keep your hops fresh by avoiding oxygen and heat: double-bag your hops and keep them in a freezer.

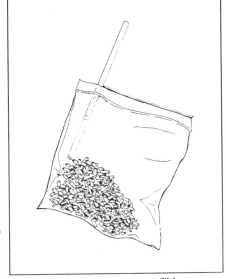

This trick works best with pellets to reduce oxidized hops.

— **This trick sucks.** When using Zip-lock™ bags to store your hops, place a plastic straw into the top of the bag. Zip the bag almost closed with just room enough for the plastic straw. Then breath in through the straw (careful not to inhale any hop fragments) until most of the oxygen is out of the bag. Pinch around the straw between taking breaths.

If done correctly you will have the bag tightly around the hops with the least amount of oxygen.

The **freshest type of hops** to buy are hop plugs. They come either vacuum packed or nitrogen bagged. Plugs are convenient to use because each one weighs a ½-ounce so you do not waste time weighing out the hops. Of course once you open the bag remember to rebag and store it in your freezer.

Tip 25: 4:00 p.m. in England— time for hop tea

This technique allows you to create great hop aroma without having to add hops directly to the fermenter. This becomes useful when transferring wort into the bottling bucket.

About 1–2 hours before you want to rack your homebrew prepare a hop tea using the following steps:

1. Add one quart of water to a medium-size, one-gallon pot and bring to a boil. Add ¼–½ ounce (or a full ounce if you *love* hops) of hop plugs or whole flower hops into a hop bag. Tie the bag closed.

2. Now toss the bag into the water and shut off the heat immediately. Do not boil the hops—just steep them. Boiling evaporates the hop bouquet you want.

3. Cover the pot and let hop bag steep for 15–20 minutes. Take bag out and place cover back on the pot.

4. Let the hop tea cool to below 70°F and, if possible, down to the temperature of the wort.

One way to speed up cooling—place the pot on a few flat frozen gel packs (the type you use in picnic coolers). Or place the covered pot in your refrigerator or freezer.

> **Caution:** Make sure the pot has cooled a bit before placing it on anything plastic.

5. You can add the hop tea when racking from primary into the secondary. Or add the hop tea when racking from secondary to your bottling bucket. Both work equally well. Experiment and see what works best.

> *Listening to your beer can help you not worry and relax. When you've heard all there is to hear, well then . . . Have a homebrew!*   – Charlie Papazian

Chapter Seven

Bottling and Kegging Pointers

Tip 26: Bottling basics

Don't boil your bottle caps—sanitize them instead in a sanitizing solution and drain them in a sanitized colander. Boiling the caps might deform the inner plastic bottle cap seal—leaving you with a flat batch of homebrew.

— **Swing-top bottles.** Save time and hassle by using Grolsch-type bottles. Scrounge them from your local recycling or bottle redemption center, ask your friends to save them, or buy the beer and save them yourself. If you can find brown swing-top bottles, use them to avoid having problems with light—as this causes skunkiness in your brew.

To sanitize—soak the bottle and the gaskets separately in sanitizer and shake dry. After several batches you might need to replace the gaskets. You can buy replacement gaskets through most homebrew suppliers.

— **Big bottles.** Champagne bottles have strong appeal. Regular crown caps fit on some champagne bottles. And obviously since they hold more liquid you will be filling less bottles (meaning less cleaning and less time spent capping).

A less apparent advantage with some champagne bottles is the bell-shaped bottom. You get a larger surface area for the yeast to settle on—resulting in a more clear homebrew.

One disadvantage with larger bottles—it is tough finishing a whole champagne bottle of India Pale Ale or Barley Wine style ale by yourself.

Solution: Simply bottle $3/4$ of your batch in champagne bottles and the other $1/4$ in regular 12-ounce bottles. This way you can enjoy a regular-size homebrew when no one else wants to split a large bottle.

— **Great storage boxes.** Ask at your nearest liquor/beer store for empty liquor or wine boxes. These boxes are great for storing beer in. They keep out light and most are fairly strong. Cut a small handle opening—one on each side—and now they are easy to carry too.

Basically, yeast farts are good for you.
— Rick Faucher, *homebrewer*

Tip 27: Great bottling tricks

Dishwasher rack. You can drip-dry your just-sanitized bottles upside-down on several sanitized dishwasher racks scrounged from old dishwashing machines. Check your local landfill for freebies.

Bottles ready and waiting. Once your beer bottles have been cleaned, sanitized, and drip-dried for bottling, you can use this technique to store them for a couple of weeks. Use a rubber band to secure a small piece of plastic wrap to the neck of each bottle. Now your bottles are ready and waiting when it comes time to bottle.

Use a bottle filler attached to your siphon tube for bottling. Various types are available (e.g., plastic or brass). Bottle fillers make it less messy than using just a rigid racking tube and flexible hose with a plastic siphon clamp attached. Plus, you will introduce less oxygen into your beer when using a bottle filler.

Brass bottle fillers are recommended over plastic ones because they are sturdier, have no spring to wear out (or lose), and last longer.

Tip 28: Perfect carbonation

For better carbonation try using dry malt extract instead of corn sugar. Most homebrewers use $2/3$–$3/4$ cup of corn sugar—instead use $3/4$–1 cup of dry malt extract. This can give your homebrew a fine bead carbonation instead of the larger bubbles you sometimes get with corn sugar.

Add the dry malt extract to a pint of warm water and boil for 5 minutes. When cooled to room temperature (i.e., 65°–70°F) pour the priming solution gently into the bottom of your bottling bucket. Carefully siphon your homebrew on top to mix in the priming solution.

> **Note:** When pouring a malt extract priming solution into your bottling bucket leave behind as much of the settled out dregs as you can. This way any protein trub from the malt will not cloud your homebrew.

Testing tip. After bottling, condition your beer at 65°–70°F for 3–4 days. Then check one bottle for the proper carbonation. If you find the batch needs more time, leave it for a few days and test again. Once the carbonation is where you want it, move the bottles to a colder place (i.e., basement or spare refrigerator).

Hydrometer reading. Always take a final gravity reading of your beer BEFORE you get ready for bottling and before you add the priming sugar. If the final gravity is too high, you need to let the fermentation continue longer. If the final gravity is too low (from where it should be) you need to add slightly more priming sugar than you would normally use.

Compare your recipe with similar beer recipes showing original gravity (O.G., also known as starting gravity) and final gravity (F.G., also known as terminal gravity). This comparison allows you to determine whether your brew is ready to be bottled.

Carbonation rule of thumb: If your homebrew started between 1.036–1.050 and your final gravity is now between 1.005–1.010, go ahead and use $^2/_3$ –$^3/_4$ cup of corn sugar (or $^3/_4$–1 cup of dry malt extract). If your homebrew starts within the same gravity range of 1.036–1.050, but ends with a gravity between 1.001 and 1.004, you probably need to use one cup of corn sugar (or 1$^1/_4$ cups of dry malt extract).

By marking the outside of your bottling bucket in 1-gallon increments, you can easily figure the amount of beer you need to bottle. If the level is less than 5 gallons after adding the priming solution, top it up to the 5-gallon mark with cooled (preboiled) water.

If you forget to check the amount of beer, you may end up with an over-carbonated beer. For example, this might happen when adding one cup of dry malt extract to only 4$^1/_4$ gallons of beer.

Conditioning temperature. Watch the temperature during the conditioning stage (when your beer is becoming carbonated). The temperature should be at 70°F for 3–4 days; then move the beer to a cooler area. If you condition between 60°–65°F, it could take as long as 2 weeks to carbonate with corn sugar. And if you primed with dried malt extract and the temperature is 60°F or lower, it could take 1–2 months to carbonate.

— **Under-carbonated homebrew?** Move your homebrew to a warmer location and give it a few more days. Test the carbonation level by sampling 1–2 bottles.

The longer you leave your homebrew in the secondary fermenter the closer it gets to a gravity of 1.000 (specific gravity of water). This is especially true with light bodied beers made using corn sugar as a fermenting additive. Be aware of this and add more sugar as needed when priming to avoid under-carbonated homebrew.

— **Over-carbonated homebrew?** Next time use less priming sugar and/or make sure the fermentation goes as far as it can. For now—when serving—try mixing your over-carbonated homebrew with a hopelessly flat homebrew in a pitcher. You will be surprised and you might have a winner on your hands! Do not tell any-one—but your best brewfriends—about your secret recipe.

Tip 29: Time-saving bottling pointers

Long boils. What do you do with your time during long boils? Sure you watch the clock. Weigh out your hops and get them ready for the hop additions. You keep an eye on the brewpot for a boilover. And you probably drink a homebrew from your last batch.

Whether you are brewing an extract batch or an all-grain batch you have to wait for the wort to boil. During this time you can bottle a previous batch.

So get your bottles cleaned and sanitized. If you keep a large, plastic trash container around with bottles soaking in a weak bleach solution, all you need to do is drain the bottles and let them drip dry.

Quick draining. When draining bottles hold them upside-down and give a couple of quick twists of the wrist. This quick spin creates a whirlpool effect which drains them TWICE as fast as just holding them upside-down.

Once boiling starts you can spend your time racking your other batch into the bottling bucket and adding the priming solution. You may be able to get about half the bottles filled and capped. Of course you still need to keep an eye on the clock, or listen for the timer for the next addition of hops or ingredients. And don't forget about *Murphy's Law of Brewing #45: The unwatched brewpot ALWAYS boils over.*

By now your brew is probably done and needs to be chilled. If you use a wort chiller you need to wait 15–20 minutes for the wort to cool down to the right temperature. This gives you some more time to finish bottling.

When you are done bottling the first batch your second batch should be done chilling. If you used an immersion type chiller, you now need to rack (transfer) your brew into the fermenter (giving you *yet* another opportunity to finish your bottling task).

Now you are DONE! You have just bottled one batch, while simultaneously brewing a second one. Of course at first it can be a little hectic. With a brew partner or enough sessions under your belt, you will soon be a *pro*!

Tip 30: Draft beer at home—
tastes great, less filling

How would you like to have creamy beer on tap—at home? You can!

The best keg to use is a 5-gallon soda keg—also called a cornelius canister. You will need a CO_2 cylinder and the necessary hookups: gas-in and liquid-out connectors, food-grade plastic tubing, adjustable metal tubing clamps, and a picnic spigot or regular bar tap.

Prepare a priming solution with $2/3$ cup of corn sugar in a boiled pint of water. Boil for 5 minutes. Let cool to 65°–70°F. Gently pour the solution into the bottom of the tall sanitized soda keg. Then rack from the secondary into the soda keg. *Pretty basic so far.*

Purge O_2 (Oxygen) with CO_2 (Carbon Dioxide). By filling your soda keg with CO_2 for 20–30 seconds you reduce the amount of oxidation that might occur when you rack your beer into the soda keg. Let the CO_2 flow in at 5 psi (pounds per square inch) with the lid off. As the beer flows in, most oxygen will be pushed out.

Seal the lid. You only need to use 5–10 pounds of CO_2 pressure to push the lid up and make a tight seal. There is a rubber O-ring on the inside of the lid. If not seated correctly, CO_2 will leak out—causing flat beer. If you hear CO_2 leaking from the lid area, pull the lid up while applying CO_2 pressure to help seal the lid.

After the lid is sealed you will want to get rid of any remaining O_2 in the keg. First release the gas pressure on the keg by pushing on the center pin (gas side) with a screwdriver. Then hook the gas connector back on and apply 5 psi till the gas stops. Repeat this 2–3 times.

Too high of a pressure can inhibit CO_2 production, so purge the soda keg—push down on the gas-in center valve—to release most of the pressure. Move the soda keg to an area 65°–70°F for 1–2 weeks of warm conditioning.

Code your lids. If you have several soda kegs it is helpful to code the lids matched to the correct kegs. Lids seal better with the original soda keg.

Cleaning stainless steel is super easy, but do not leave chlorine solutions in it for more than a few hours. Over time this might cause pits or even small holes in your precious soda kegs.

Try to get sanitizer into the gas-in and liquid-out connectors. If you remembered to clean it out just after you last used it, the keg should be fairly easy to sanitize. Sometimes it is worth filling the keg with a sanitizer, sealing the lid, and running sanitizer through the liquid-out side to completely clean the long dip tube.

> **Note:** When sanitizing the soda keg be sure to remove the rubber O-ring and completely sanitize it.

Sometimes **used soda kegs** have been kicked around and are dented. This makes for *tricky* kegging. If you are buying a used soda keg check the lid area for dents or buy a new one (if you can afford it). This can save you a lot of time and hassle.

After 1–2 weeks move your beer to a cooler place (i.e., basement or spare refrigerator). If you place the keg in a cold refrigerator (i.e., 40°–50°F) use about 8–14 psi on the beer. If you moved the keg to a cool basement or closet (i.e., 50°–60°F) use about 14–22 psi.

Adjust the gas toward the lower end of either range if you have an ale on tap. If you are serving your friends a lager, adjust the gas toward the higher end for a tad more carbonation. *Let the beer flow!*

Homebrew on draft anyone?

Chapter Eight

Secrets from Fellow Homebrewers

Tip 31: Avoid off-flavors caused by improper fermentation

Slow fermentation can cause **sulfurlike aromas** in your final beer. Hydrogen sulfide is produced when your homebrew is left on the yeast sediment for too long at warm temperatures. And you can also get a yeasty taste (called yeast bite) by not racking soon enough after primary fermentation is over.

Basic rules. Do not leave your homebrew on a large amount of yeast for more than 3–4 days. After primary fermentation has slowed down and yeast sediment has finished accumulating (e.g., within 4–5 days from start of fermentation), transfer your homebrew to the secondary fermenter. Or if you have reached the final gravity your recipe and style calls for, bottle the beer.

Watch your fermenting temperatures. Lagers are happy between 35°–50°F. Ales work best between 60°–70°F. Any lower or higher in these ranges and you may have slow or off-flavor fermentations.

Tip 32: Warm weather fermentation tricks

These inexpensive and proven methods work great for fermenting ales during hot weather.

— Cool it. If you have a central air conditioning system set your fermenter on the floor so it covers half the floor vent. Next make a paper bag large enough to fit over the fermenter and the vent. By using a few grocery bags and some masking tape, you can easily make your own bag. Or buy a large brown-paper lawn bag found in some hardware or lawn and garden stores.

— Scary noises in the closet? Place your fermenter in a large, clean plastic garbage barrel or laundry tub (new if possible) in the coolest part of your house or apartment. Consider placing the barrel in a dark closet to get it out of the way.

What to do with the spent grains? Put them in a bowl outside and let the birds enjoy.
— Jim Trautwein, Homebrewer's Software

Fill the barrel with cold water to half the height of the fermenter. Fill several plastic 2-liter soda bottles with water, twist the caps on, and place them in your freezer. In the morning, and at night, place 1–2 newly frozen bottles around the fermenter. Be sure to keep the barrel lid closed to keep the cold in. Maybe even throw a colorful blanket over the whole thing for aesthetics or more importantly (*we're homebrewers, we don't care about aesthetics*) to keep the cold in and the hot out.

— **Cool water wick.** If you do not have room in your freezer to freeze the bottles (or do not want to bother), drape a towel around the top of the fermenter with part of the towel hanging into the cold water. The towel acts as a water wick.

As the water slowly evaporates it keeps the fermenter cool. To keep the fermenter between 60°–70°F—throw ice cubes in the ice water bath as needed. Be sure to monitor temperature daily using a thermometer floating in the water bath.

Caution: Test the leakability of your ice water tub/ barrel outside your home first. A pin-hole or crack would cause a BIG mess if it leaked.

When introducing someone to homebrewed beer don't serve 'the-strongest-one-you've-ever-made' to the poor guy. The shock will often put him OFF homebrew. — *The Beersmith*, Louisiana

Tip 33: Cold weather fermentation tricks

For some homebrewers, winter makes it challenging to keep fermentation temperatures under control. These cold weather tips will help.

— **Heat with light.** Place a lamp or light bulb in a cabinet or small closet with your fermenter. By changing the wattage of the light bulb you can control the temperature of the fermentation. Be careful to keep the bulb away from anything flammable.

Instead of changing different wattage light bulbs—install a dimmer switch. Now you can easily adjust the wattage by turning a dimmer knob to control temperature.

— **Bundle up your fermenter** with blankets and/or insulation. Either styrofoam or even the newer plastic-wrapped pink house insulation work equally well.

Try lining all sides (and the bottom) of an appropriately sized cardboard box with rigid insulation. Cut a hole in the bottom of the box for the airlock to poke through. Place the box, upside-down, over the fermenter. This setup saves you the effort of having to lift your fermenter in and out of your insulated box.

Contrary to popular belief, B-Brite™ *is not a sanitizer. It is only a cleanser.*
— David and Lisa Hoffmann, *The Brewmeister*

Tip 34: Reduce oxidation and loss of hop flavor/aroma

Rack gently. Do not splash your homebrew or wort when transferring it from one container to another as this may reduce hop aroma.

Place an **adjustable metal hose clamp** over the joint where the racking hose and the bottle filler meet. This way you prevent oxygen from creeping in during siphoning.

Starting the flow. When wort starts to flow from the racking hose into an empty fermenter or bucket, make sure the tube is long enough to lay flat in the bottom of the container.

Tip the container (almost 45° from horizontal) so that within the first several seconds the end of the siphon tube is under the liquid. Once the liquid is high enough gently lower the container back to level without sloshing.

An alternative technique is to keep the flow of the wort very slow until the liquid level has reached two inches from the bottom. You can easily control the speed of the flow by opening and closing a plastic hose clamp attached to your racking hose.

This attention to not splashing saves your homebrew from oxygenation and allows the hop flavor and bouquet to come through in your finished homebrew.

Kegging equipment. If you have a CO_2 cylinder handy, create a CO_2 environment in the receiving container. From the CO_2 cylinder run the gas hose into the bottom of your empty container (with the lid off). Turn the CO_2 gas on at 5 psi. Once you start to smell CO_2 (or after 15–20 seconds) turn off the CO_2.

Now you can easily rack your homebrew into the fermenter without worrying about oxygen. As the liquid level rises the CO_2 will push the O_2 out.

Use special oxygen-absorbing bottle caps available through the American Homebrewers' Association, Boulder, Colorado (303) 447-0816. These bottle caps are designed to absorb any oxygen present in the headspace above your homebrew after you have capped it.

Tip 35: High-alcohol beers— perfect every time

One problem you might have when fermenting high alcohol (or high original gravity) beers is having a stuck or slow fermentation. This can result from not enough oxygen being present, or from using a low-alcohol tolerant yeast strain.

Aeration—shake it, don't break it. After pitching the yeast, shake the wort for 2–3 minutes every half-hour over a 2–3 hour period. This gives your wort enough oxygen to make your high-alcohol beer keep on chugging. Aeration is important to low-alcohol beers too, but is harder to achieve with high-gravity worts.

Another problem with high gravity worts is not having the right amount of nutrients for a strong fermentation. Adding yeast nutrients (energizers) can help.

Scotty. . .ENERGIZE. High gravity and light beers benefit from the added nutrition of one tsp. of yeast energizer per 5-gallons and creates a more complete fermentation. Add yeast energizer 5 minutes before end of boil.

Hop more. You must also pay attention to the amount of hops you use for bittering a strong beer. The tendency is to under-hop during brewing, but you should add *more* bittering hops than you think.

As your original gravity (O.G.) goes up you need to add more hops to balance out your homebrew. The hopping level for a Bock (O.G.: 1.080°) is not just twice the hopping level of a Bitter (O.G.: 1.040°). In fact it will be *more than* twice. This is because as the density of the wort increases, the amount of hop bitterness you can extract (hop utilization) decreases.

Follow recipes carefully; make sure you have enough hops; and boil highly hopped worts long enough (i.e., $1-1\frac{1}{2}$ hours) to dissolve the hop oils.

Tough yeast. Make sure you use an alcohol tolerant yeast strain, or even wine yeast.

Liquor in the airlock. Whenever you are fermenting a beer longer than a normal period of time (i.e., more than 3 weeks) add either vodka or a similar high alcohol liquor in the airlock. This prevents any kind of nasty bacteria from growing over a period of several months. Do not worry if you get a little bit of alcohol in your beer—the taste is negligible.

Tip 36: In the dark?— keep it that way

Keep your homebrew from getting a light-struck (skunky) taste by wrapping an old (but clean) sweatshirt or towel completely covering your carboy during fermentation. The darker the shirt or towel the better. You can even use an old blanket, pillowcase, or large paper bag.

Use the same rule with your finished bottled beer. When storing your beer in a room with a window, try to place the beer far away from the window. Throw a blanket on top if you do not have cases with tops.

Tip 37: Toasting and smoking grains

Have you ever made a casserole or stew for dinner and put the leftovers away in the refrigerator? After eating the leftovers a couple of days later you say, "Wow. This taste's even better now!" The same works with toasting and smoking malt grains.

Toasting. When brewing an English India Pale Ale, for example, you might want to toast some pale malt to create an authentic taste. You can toast uncracked malt grains by baking them on cookie sheets (1–2 grains deep) in a 350°F oven for 10–15 minutes.

Smoking. To create a German Rauchbier you will need to smoke the grains on an outdoor grill using hickory or maple wood chips. Uncracked malt grains can be placed on a cookie sheet (1–2 grains deep) and smoked for 5–10 minutes. Clean window screens work well too.

Soak in the flavor. It is better to toast—or smoke— the uncracked grains and store them for a couple of weeks in a Tupperware™ container. Then crack the malt grains just before you need to use them.

This technique lets the full flavor of the grains develop.

Tip 38: Better head retention

Add a little malted wheat into your recipes and your homebrew will have better head retention.

In your next brew use 1–2 cups of wheat malt grain (in an all-grain batch) or up to a pound of wheat malt extract syrup. This low amount of wheat does not alter the taste of your homebrew but definitely improves head stability.

When you open a 3- to 4-lb. can of wheat malt extract and dip out one pound, you need to save the rest for your next brew session. To keep it clean—wrap a clean plastic bag on top with an elastic band holding it in place (or use the plastic lid if the can came with one). Now place the can in the freezer until you need to brew with it.

Just remember to thaw the can of wheat malt by taking it out of the freezer one day before you brew. Heat the can of malt in a large cooking pot filled with hot water a couple of inches below the top of the can.

With all-grain brewing, the addition of $\frac{1}{2}$–1 pound of oats to the grist also helps with head retention.

Tip 39: Making great fruit beer without a lot of mess

Sometimes homebrewers brew with adjuncts—anything fermentable you add to your beer which contributes mouth-feel, taste, aroma, and/or fermentable sugars.

You can use fruit as an adjunct by pasteurizing the fruit and placing it in the primary or secondary fermenter. Pasteurize by boiling $1/2$-gallon of water, shutting off the heat, adding the fruit, and steeping it for 30 minutes. Do NOT boil. Boiling fruit causes permanent haze.

Be sure the beer ends up with just the hint of the fruit used. When too much fruit is used it can be too sweet and/or tart—and very tough to drink. About 5–8 pounds per 5-gallon batch is probably enough for most types of fruit. Experiment and find out what works best.

Avoid fruit in the primary. With all the CO_2 being expelled from the primary fermenter you can lose most of those great fruit aromas!

Soda/pop kegs. It is recommended to place fruit in a stainless steel secondary fermenter so that you can easily reach in and pull out a fruit-filled muslin bag. Plus, soda kegs give you the least amount of clogging trouble.

> **Note:** When cleaning out your soda keg after a fruit fermentation—make sure you completely flush out the dip tube. Fruit pulp may have crept up the tube.

Caution: Do NOT use a glass carboy when fermenting a fruit beer. The fruit could clog up and become dangerous (either by shooting a high pressure spray of gunk, or by cracking and even exploding the glass carboy).

Frozen fruit. The best fruit to use is frozen fruit because it is frozen fresh. All you need to do is pasteurize it and add it to your brew.

If using fresh (unfrozen) fruit you must first crush the fruit so the juices will flow. With frozen fruit the freezing process has already crushed the skin.

Brew a light-colored homebrew. The lighter the malt used the better because you want to see the color and taste the flavor of the fruit in your beer.

Fruit juice concentrate. A simple and effective way to brew a fruit beer is to use juice concentrates. For example, Knudson 8-ounce black cherry juice concentrate can be added to your wort just after the boil is done. Or buy specially prepared fruit concentrates for homebrewing. Just pasteurize the fruit concentrate for 15–20 minutes (no boiling) before adding it to the brewpot. Try brewing a honey lager with this—it is excellent!

To pasteurize fruit:

1. Add 2–3 quarts of water to a 2-gallon cooking pot.

2. Bring to a boil.

3. Shut off heat and drop a large fruit-filled muslin bag into the pot.

4. Steep for 30 minutes with the cover on.

5. Let the fruit mixture cool (covered in your refrigerator or freezer) until the temperature drops to between 65° and 70°F.

> **Note:** Do not boil the fruit or fruit pectin comes out and may cause haze problems in your beer.

Next, using sanitized rubber gloves, squeeze as much liquid as possible out of the fruit-filled muslin bag into the brewpot. Remove the bag and pour the fruit liquid into the secondary fermenter. Then rack from the primary into the secondary.

At this point, if you are using a glass carboy, throw the leftover fruit pulp into your compost bin. By steeping you have extracted a good part of the flavor of the fruit.

If you are using a soda keg as a secondary fermenter, you can also add the fruit bag to the fermenter. After pasteurizing the fruit add 20–25 large, sanitized marbles to help keep the fruit-filled hop bag submerged in the soda keg. Several sanitized spoons work well too.

Concentrated wort. It is advisable to brew a concentrated wort so you should end up with just 3–4 gallons of wort in the primary. After combining the wort with the fruit and boiled water in the secondary you should end up with a total of 5 gallons of wort.

Finings. When brewing fruit beers it is important to add gelatin finings (a clarification substance which helps yeast and proteins settle to the bottom) 8–10 days before bottling.

Top it up. If you end up with less than 5 gallons of beer after adding priming sugar and racking the beer into the bottling bucket, top it up with preboiled water to the correct level.

Priming. With most fruit beers, use a little more than the regular amount of priming sugar (e.g., one cup of corn sugar or $1\frac{1}{4}$ cup of dry malt extract). The more carbonation there is, the more fruit aromas will be released for you and your friends to enjoy!

Tip 40: Easy labeling and delabeling

Labeling. Use milk as a glue when labeling your homebrew bottles. Float a label face-up for a few seconds in a shallow bowl of milk. Apply your label to a bottle and use a towel to tamp dry. Repeat steps for the remaining bottles.

When it comes time to getting the labels off—simply soak the bottles in hot water for several seconds and off they come. No chemicals and no scrubbing!

Is labeling your homebrew bottles a chore? After awhile labeling 40–60 bottles per batch can become a *pain*. And coming up with a new and creative label design *every* time can be difficult too.

The only thing that's more fun than making a good beer is drinking it.   — Dave Miller,
                  author of *Brewing the World's Great Beers*

Instead of creating a new label every time create a standard (but very special) label. Whether you make your own labels by hand or with a computer, it can be fun. Or if you know a good artist, offer a 6-pack of your best homebrew in return for an excellent master label.

The **master label** should be fairly large and then reduced to the correct size. This technique gives your labels good clarity. Size the master for 12-ounce bottles at 3 in. by 3¾ in. and for 22-ounce bottles at 3½ in. by 4 in. Make six copies of each size master. Then cut and paste each size onto separate 8½ in. by 11 in. sheets of paper. You now have master sheets for each size bottle ready for photocopying.

Be sure to leave a blank area where you can handwrite the name of the style or particular name of the current batch. You can even photocopy the master sheets on different colored paper (i.e., dark brown for Porters and Stouts, white for Weissbier and Weizen, yellow for Pale Ales, etc.).

By color-coding the labels to match the homebrew, you can quickly identify your beers: *"Honey, grab us a Porter please!"*

— **Save even more time.** Just label two 6-packs out of every batch. On the non-labeled bottles write the batch number with a fine-tip permanent marker on the bottlecaps. Use non-labeled bottles for competitions and house beer (your own use). Use your gorgeously labeled bottles when having friends and family over, or when bringing your brew to parties and club meetings.

Of course you still might want to design a special label once a year for that once-in-a-lifetime occasion, or for your annual Christmas beer.

— Delabel glued-on commercial bottle labels with a solution of $\frac{1}{2}$ cup of ammonia to 5 gallons of hot water. After soaking bottles for 10–15 minutes paper labels will float off. Foil labels may take 20–25 minutes to come off.

Apologies to the St. Pauli Girl. (Art by Julie Weisberg)

Four to five days after bottling, give each bottle (sitting in the beer case) a quick spin in "one" direction. This sets up a "mini" whirlpool in each bottle that helps drop sediment out of solution.
                                    – Glenn Roy, Beer Essentials

Max's Own
Hog
Grog...Makes
you squeal
like a pig!

Chapter Nine

Traditional, All-Grain Brewing Demystified

Tip 41: Basic all-grain brewing (mashing)

All-grain brewing really is *not* complicated. And once you get the hang of it—and shorten the time it takes—all-grain brewing can be a lot of fun. Some people enjoy the time it takes because it gives them a chance to relax and read the Sunday paper during the process.

Infusion mashing (just one of several mashing techniques)—Overview. You add cracked malt grains to water at a specific temperature for a certain period of time. When you start the grain is a starch. When you finish, the grains will have been converted (with a little help from diastatic enzymes) into fermentable sugars and dextrins (unfermentables contributing mouth-feel). Next you raise the temperature for a short time to end the conversion process. After sparging (or rinsing) the grains with hot water to extract the sweet wort, you are done and ready for the boil!

Here is an all-around useful mash procedure and timing schedule:

1. Use 1.33 quarts of mash water to each pound of grain (including malt grains, adjuncts, and specialty grains such as caramel) you plan to use. Add filtered and/or preboiled tap water to a 33-quart enamel canning pot and turn heat on. This size pot takes up two burners on a typical stovetop or fits nicely on a separate propane burner stand (sometimes called a Cajun burner).

2. Crack the malt grains (while the mash water is heating up) using a hand corona mill or roller mill. Do not crack or mill the malt too finely or you might have sparging runoff (wort draining from lauter tun) problems.

When grinding dark malts, such as black patent or chocolate, it is better to grind them to a course powder. You will not need to use as much dark malts and your final homebrew will be noticeably smoother. When you finish grinding the dark malts remember to readjust the grinding plates of a corona mill or set the rollers of a roller-type grinder back to a wider setting for the next time you grind lighter grains.

3. Add the malt grains into the mash tun (the vessel where mashing occurs) when the strike (starting) temperature of the mash water reaches 10°–12°F higher than the desired rest temperature. Stir slowly at first until the grain dust calms down. Then stir quickly to get an even temperature distribution. Make sure all the malt grain gets completely wet.

4. Take a temperature reading from the center of the mash tun once the mash has been evenly distributed. If necessary turn on the heat to boost your mash to the desired conversion temperature. Keep the mash at a specific temperature between 146°–159°F (conversion temperature range) for 30–75 minutes.

> **Note:** The higher the temperature you hold the conversion at, the more dextrins (unfermentables contributing mouth-feel and body) your homebrew will have.

What temperature is best for conversion? This depends on the type of malt grain you are mashing with and the beer style you are brewing. Some malt grains have a high level of diastatic enzymes (which convert starches into sugars and dextrins).

Use the following as a rough guideline:

Malt Grain Type	Temp. Conversion Range
German (2-row)	150°-151°F
English (2-row)	150°-151°F
Klages (2-row)	154°-155°F
Domestic (6-row)	158°-159°F

How long to hold the rest temperature for? A basic rule of thumb is to mash for at least 60–75 minutes. However, with most malt grain you might have conversion within 20–30 minutes. If you decide to decrease the mash time (to save time) you should do an iodine test to make sure the conversion from starches to sugars and dextrins has occurred.

Iodine test. Place a couple of tablespoons of the mash liquid on a white saucer and let cool to room temperature. Then use a drop or two of tincture of iodine (available in pharmacies) to stain the mash sample. If starches are still present it will change to blue-black indicating you will need to continue the rest for another 10–15 minutes.

Keep taking an iodine test (cleaning off the spoon between samplings) until the iodine color does *not* turn blue-black. At this point conversion has happened and you can begin the mash-out (or mash-off) stage.

Temperature control is very important because fluctuations of 1–2 degrees can change your final homebrew. If you are using an uninsulated mash kettle you need to apply heat every 30 minutes for about a minute. And stir every 15 minutes for no more than one minute (spoon in one hand and thermometer in the other hand).

Watch out for overshooting your desired temperature. The mash has a lag time so turn off the heat 3–5 degrees before you reach the desired temperature. Keep a pint of cold water handy—in case you overshoot the rest temperature—so you can throw it in.

Insulated mash tun (i.e., picnic cooler). It is best to preheat the walls of a picnic cooler by adding the necessary amount of 180°F mash water into the cooler. Check the temperature until it drops to about 10°–12°F higher than the desired rest temperature. Then slowly add the grains to the cooler/mash tun while stirring.

After adding all the grist (grain and adjuncts) the temperature should be close to the rest temperature.

Once you get the mash to the correct temperature (using an insulated mash tun) it should remain within 1°–2°F for the duration of the conversion. However, you should still stir at 30-minute intervals.

5. Check the pH level as soon as you reach the right rest temperature. The diastatic enzymes in the grain need a mash pH level of 5.2–5.4 to do their job properly. Using a large sanitized, stainless steel spoon, skim a small sample (i.e., 1–2 tablespoons) of wort (avoiding solids) off the top of the mash. Let cool for 2–3 minutes down to 60°F then dip a pH testing paper into the sample. Compare the color of the paper to the pH color chart provided with your test kit. If possible view under natural lighting in front of a white background.

If the pH is higher than 5.4, adjust by adding ½ teaspoon of gypsum to the mash and stir into the mash completely. Wait a few minutes and test the pH again. If still too high, repeat as necessary. Do not add more than ½ teaspoon at any given addition. And do not add more than 2 teaspoons total. A pH level between 5.0–5.3 is best.

6. Mash-out. The last step is to boost the heat to 165°–168°F for 5 minutes. This step is called mash-out and you are stopping all enzymatic processes dead in their tracks.

When using a large metal mash tun—just boost the temperature with heat from your stovetop.

If using the picnic cooler method—add two quarts (one pint at a time) of 180°F water. Stir and check temperature between water additions. Stop adding water when the mash temperature reaches 165°–168°F and hold for five minutes.

7. Lautering. Now you are ready for the lautering process where hot sparge water rinses the grains to extract the sweet wort.

See Tip 43 for details on lautering.

Tip 42: Controlling mash temperature

During the mash (when you are converting the starches to fermentable sugars and dextrins) you must keep the temperature constant within 1°–2°F. Here are a few pointers on how to do this.

— Use a large 34-quart (or 44-quart) picnic cooler. They make great mash tuns because they are so well insulated. After you get your mash to the correct temperature, close the top. The temperature should stay steady for one hour or more. Take a quick temperature check every half-hour to be sure. (Leave your thermometer centered in the mash.)

— **Low oven heat.** If you mash in a large canning pot or large stainless steel vessel, preheat your oven to 120°–140°F. Make room in your oven by removing all but one rack (set to the lowest level). If the mash tun still doesn't fit, remove the rack and let the pot sit on the bottom of the oven. **Note:** This may not work if you have an electric oven.

When your mash gets to the right temperature, place your mash tun in the oven.

To be safe use an oven thermometer to make sure the oven heating dial is accurate. Otherwise you may think you are at 140°F, but really be at 200°F!

Once you place the mash tun in and close the oven door you can turn the heat completely off.

Every 15 minutes stir and check the temperature. If it is too low, boost on the stovetop (not with oven heat). And if the temperature is too high—add some cold brewing water (preboiled and cooled water).

— **Build an insulated mash tun cabinet.** You might be lucky enough to have a large storage box or find one at a garage or tag sale. Install a light fixture and light bulb in the back or top of the box. Assuming you are using a brewpot as your mash tun, place the brewpot in the box during the mash conversion.

A mash tun cabinet will keep the temperature constant. Boosting of the mash temperature is done on the stove.

Tip 43: The basics of using a lauter tun

When using a two-bucket lauter tun system you should remember a few important things.

— **Sparge water.** The correct amount of sparge water (hot water used to rinse the grains in the lauter tun) can be easily calculated for a 5-gallon batch size using the following formula:

Amount of sparge water = 7 gallons – amount of mash water used (1.33 quarts per pounds of grains and adjuncts used rounded to nearest quart)

For example, when brewing a batch with ten pounds of grains and adjuncts, you will need 13 quarts of mash water. Using the formula above:

28 quarts (7 gallons) – 13 quarts (1.33 x 10 quarts) of mash water = 15 quarts of sparge water.

— **To save time:** During the mash stage heat the needed amount of sparge water to 160°–168°F.

— **Adjust the pH level** to 5.5–5.7 with gypsum using the procedures used in the mashing stage above.

By getting the pH level close to 5.5–5.7 pH you are avoiding any off-flavors (i.e., astringency) which may result during the sparging process.

— **The set up.** Place your lauter tun on a countertop with the hose resting in the bottom of your brewpot. Position the empty brewpot on the floor or on a chair so it is lower than the lauter tun. Keep the pot with the sparge water on low heat to maintain 165°–168°F.

A better way is to put the empty brewpot on the stovetop and position the lauter tun higher. An empty case of beer can be used to hold the lauter tun. This way you will not have to move your brewpot once it is full. *See photo on page 111.*

To reduce the amount of wort left behind in the lauter tun, place a one-foot piece of 2 by 4 lumber under the bucket (opposite side from spigot) to tilt it forward.

Cross-section of inner bucket in a two-bucket lauter system.

—**Foundation water.** Fill the bottom of the lauter tun with 170°–175° water (foundation water) 3–4 inches above the bottom of the top bucket. This should be done just before you start adding any mash grains into the lauter vessel. By doing this you avoid chances of a stuck runoff (when the flow of wort stops).

Now gently add the mash grains into the bottom of the lauter tun. A one-quart measuring pitcher works fine. You can use a small saucepan too.

Alternate adding mash grains and part of the sparge water. The liquid level should always be above the grains.

Wait 5–10 minutes for the mash to settle before starting the runoff.

—Recycle the first runoff. Turn on the spigot or open the siphon clamp ¼ open and there you go! Pour sparge water gently (or sprinkle it if you can) on the mash surface. Recycle the first ½-gallon back to the top of the grain bed to get a clear runoff. When the flow from the hose shows no grain husks coming through, stop recycling the wort. In fact, if the wort immediately runs clear— there is no need to recycle it.

> **Note**: The wort runoff should flow very slowly. The whole process may take 40–50 minutes depending on the amount of grains used.

Avoid stuck runoffs. Never allow the liquid level to drop below the top of grains. You want to suspend the grains throughout sparging so the filter bed does not get compacted and slow (or stop) the runoff. When you run out of sparge water, of course you just let it drain.

Do not over sparge! When trying to get a higher quantity of wort (than is normal) you may extract harsh tannins and lower the specific gravity of your homebrew. When the runoff becomes very cloudy or the specific gravity drops below 1.005—IMMEDIATELY stop the sparging.

Once sparging is complete the inner bucket containing spent grains can be lifted out—ready for cleaning.

The liquid level of the wort in the brewpot should be six gallons. If not, top up with preboiled water. At least a $\frac{1}{2}$ gallon should evaporate during the boil (if not, boil harder). But how do you measure liquid flowing into your brewpot?

To estimate the amount of wort in your brewpot you need to calculate the number of inches per gallon (i.p.g.) for that particular brewpot. To calculate i.p.g. first pour exactly two gallons of water into your brewpot. Then, using a plastic ruler, measure from the bottom (and middle) of the pot to the top of the liquid level. Divide this number by two and this is your i.p.g. factor. When runoff is complete, measure the liquid level with your cleaned and sanitized ruler and divide by the i.p.g. factor to get the number of gallons in the brewpot. Top up with preboiled water as needed.

Now you are ready to start the boil. Have *fun*!

Always use the freshest ingredients!
— Matt, *Barleymalt and Vine*

Tip 44: All-grain brewing—tips to save you time and money

First, try to find a helpful brewing partner. This will pass the time and make it quicker to get things done. If you cannot find one (or bribe one with some of the final brew), here are a few things you can do to speed things up.

— **If you have chlorinated tap water,** it is important to prepare your brewing water (used for mashing and sparging). Boiling for a $\frac{1}{2}$-hour and then cooling water overnight gets rid of any chlorine in the water.

— **Grain grinding.** The biggest problem homebrewers have when first doing all-grain brewing is having a stuck runoff. This is when the filtering bed of grains collapses and the wort stops flowing. How you grind the malt affects the flow of the wort.

There are three devices used for grinding: kitchen rolling pin (messy, time-consuming, not consistent, cheap); corona mill (fairly fast, trial and error to adjust correctly, moderately priced); and roller-type grinder (fastest, easier to adjust to the right level, more expensive).

Do not grind to a fine powder. You should crack the grain so the husks are crushed, but not pulverized. You should still be able to see husks fairly intact after grinding. White chunks of the grains' endosperm should be showing. Some fine flour will be present—but not much.

If you are still unsure of what the cracked grains should be like, visit a local homebrew shop or micro-brewery. Chances are they can show you some cracked grains.

Crank it up! If your grain grinder does not fit on a regular countertop—then use a ladder.

— **Double-batching.** Ever wonder how some homebrewers have such a well-stocked selection of their homeys? Some homebrewers double-batch brew.

They use one lauter tun and twice as much grain for a 5-gallon batch. Then they brew two batches at the same time!

Here is how to double-batch brew:

Take your first runnings (first 3–4 gallons of runoff) for a high gravity beer (i.e., 1.080–1.100). Then use another 4–5 gallons of sparge water (second runnings) and get enough wort for a low gravity homebrew (i.e., Mild Ale or Bitter at 1.035–1.040).

Of course you need two brewpots, more stovetop burner area, and two fermenters available at the same time.

Double-batching takes a little more time than a regular brew session for a 5-gallon batch. But it does not take twice as long!

> **Important:** If you oversparge your second batch, your homebrew could end up pretty thin and you might even get some harsh tannins. To avoid this— make sure your sparge water is adjusted to 5.7 pH. Discontinue the sparge when the specific gravity of the wort drops below 1.005.

— **Double-batch variation.** Take the first runnings for a high gravity homebrew. Then, when going through another run of sparge water, use only $2\frac{1}{2}$ gallons. Make up the rest of the malt needed for the second batch by adding 3–4 pounds of malt extract and enough water to bring the liquid level up to six gallons. After a full-wort batch is finished boiling, a $\frac{1}{2}$-gallon or more of liquid will have evaporated (which is what you want).

— **Timing tip.** One piece of equipment you do not need two of is the wort chiller. If you stagger the two batches by 30 minutes you can use the wort chiller on batch #1 while batch #2 is boiling. When batch #1 is done chilling, batch #2 will be ready for the wort chiller.

— **Cool and dry.** Avoid storing grain in damp basements. Instead store grain some place cool and dry (maybe in a closet). This keeps bacteria and other contaminants out.

Double-wrap the grain in heavy-duty plastic bags. And use rubber/plastic storage bins (with lids) to store your bagged grain.

—Pre-ground malt grain. The best way to ensure you have the correct grind is to have your grains pre-ground by your friendly homebrew supplier. This also saves you the time and hassle of grinding your own (and buying a grinding mill). Make sure you use up what you buy within six months or else your malt may get a little stale.

Patience is a virtue, especially when homebrewing. Don't rush. Let nature brew your beer.
                    – Barney Brower, *Adirondack Brewing Supply*

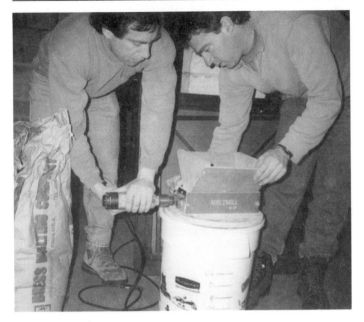

Professional brewers, Tony (L) and Pete (R) Poanessa at Elm City Brewing Company's pilot brewery. A roller-type mill (MaltMill^{TM}) and attached electric drill make for quick and easy grinding!

The night before you brew, put all your equipment that will fit into a 7.5-gallon plastic bucket in a sanitizing solution. This saves you hours of preparatory cleaning.

—Matthew Price, Harrisville homebrewer

Chapter Ten

Homemade Brewing Gadgets

Tip 45: Build an immersion wort chiller

An immersion wort chiller uses a long coil of copper tubing which is immersed in the hot wort. Cold water flows through the coil absorbing the heat from the wort. This type of chiller has the advantage of being easy to build and easy to clean.

Materials needed:

– 25 feet of $\frac{3}{8}$ in. inner diameter (I.D.) copper refrigeration tubing

– one garden hose coupling that ends in a hose barb for $\frac{1}{2}$ in. I.D. plastic hose

– enough ½ in. I.D. food-grade plastic tubing to reach
   from your sink to your brew stove and back again

– 3 small adjustable hose clamps that will clamp ½–¾
   in. pipes

How to build an immersion wort chiller:

1. Coil the copper tubing around a circular form so the
diameter of the coil is a couple of inches less than the
smallest pot you plan to use the chiller in.

2. Using a tubing bender, bend the ends of the tubing
so they protrude over the top of the tallest pot you plan
to use this chiller in. You may want to hook the ends over
the edge of the pot so any cold water leaks do not go into
your brewpot.

3. Cut the plastic hose in half. Attach one end of each
piece to the ends of the copper coil (one inch up on the
pipe). Secure the tubing with metal hose clamps.

4. Attach the garden hose coupling to one of the plastic
tubes. Secure this joint with a hose clamp. Using a rubber
band, secure the 2 hoses together one foot or so from the
end farthest from the chiller. This keeps the output hose
from sliding out of the sink.

Using your chiller— About 15 minutes before the
end of your boil, plop the chiller into your boiling wort
to sanitize it. At the end of the boil connect the hose
coupling to your sink (you may need a sink garden hose
attachment). Make sure the output end is in the sink. As
you turn on the water keep an eye on the output end as
it may flop around when the water comes on.

Once the wort is at or below 70°F, turn off the water. You are now ready to rack the wort into your fermenter and pitch your yeast.

[Source: Greg & Lynne Lawrence, *Lil' Olde Wine-making Shoppe*]

Easy to build and use! Just plop it in 15 minutes before the end of boil. Julie Weisberg in her homebrewery.

To clean: As soon as you pitch the yeast and get the airlock in place—clean your chiller. If you wash it off with hot water soon after use, you can easily get it clean. If you wait too long (i.e., several hours or overnight) you may have to boil some water to get it clean.

If you brew full 5-gal. batches, you may want to use 40 ft. of tubing instead of 25 ft. This shortens the cooling time, *but* increases the cost of your wort chiller.]

Tip 46: Where's my brew blanket??!!

After a messy brew session do you spend time cleaning and mopping your brewing area floor? Instead find an old wool blanket to put down on your kitchen floor before you begin to brew. While brewing a batch you are sure to drop or spill something (i.e., wort, malt, or hops).

When your brew session is over—just shake the blanket out in your backyard or into a garbage can. Then throw your brew blanket in the wash.

To clean the blanket you probably want to wash it by itself. And if you are brewing an all-grain batch, make sure to clean out your clothes washer filter afterward—or you might get grain accumulating in the filter.

> **Note:** Make sure the blanket lays flat on the floor. Place something heavy on each corner to keep the blanket flat. You do not want to trip carrying something hot or heavy!

> *Add one pound of Panella (Mexican Brown) sugar to your Trappist recipe for a surprisingly authentic taste.*
> —Brian Wood, *Lubbock Homebrew*

Tip 47 (part 1): An effective all-grain lauter tun for less than $15

First, you need to get two large food-grade plastic buckets—a local donught shop might provide you with these for roughly $1 each. Ask for the large 5-gallon size with a lid.

You also need a $1/16$-in. drill bit, a one-inch hole saw bit, an electric drill, a plastic spigot (with washer and locking nut; your local homebrew shop should be able to sell you one for a few bucks), and a length of $3/8$-in. outer diameter food-grade plastic hose.

Chances are you can use your existing siphon hose to attach to the spigot. But if you need some more hose, you should be able to get some at your homebrew shop.

That's all you need! Now here is what you do:

1. Wash both buckets with water and detergent. Remove any labels—it may take a few times washing to completely remove the labels.

Attaching a siphon hose to a bottle washer...will allow you to fill buckets and fermenters with aerated water...important to the first stages of yeast growth.
    –Jon Scanlon, *Hops & Things*

2. Turn one bucket upside-down, get your drill (with a $\frac{1}{16}$-in. bit) and find a comfortable chair to sit on while you drill. This *may* take a while.

3. Now drill between 200–300 holes in the bottom of the bucket. No need to count—just go nuts.

Top bucket with 200-300 holes drilled.

4. Now get the other bucket (this will be the outer bucket of the lauter tun) and mark on the outside of the bucket $1\frac{1}{2}$ inches from the bottom—this is to be the center of the hole to be drilled by the one-inch hole saw.

5. Go ahead—drill that hole!

6. Now the spigot can be fitted into the second bucket. Place the washer on the spigot before placing it in the new hole. Reach inside, twist lock nut on, and turn tight.

7. Finally, fit the length of tubing onto the end of the spigot and you are ready for use.

[Source: Chris Heatley, co-founding member of *N.H. Biernuts* homebrew club]

Tip 47 (part 2): Insulating your lauter tun

It is helpful to insulate your lauter tun in order to keep the temperature constant. It may take as long 40–50

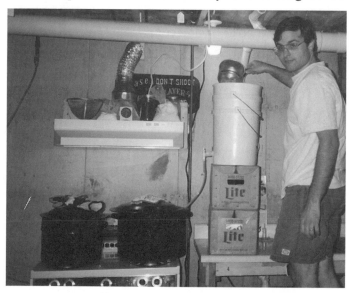

Author and his 2-bucket lauter tun system.

minutes to completely sparge the grains with hot water. The colder the mash, the more runoff problems you can have.

To easily make your own insulated jacket—use a cardboard box and rigid 2-in. thick insulation on all sides (inside or outside). If you are concerned about little foam insulation fragments finding their way into your homebrew, place each of the 6 pieces (e.g., 4 sides, top, and bottom) into 6 separate plastic bags. Then tape the bags shut using duct tape (*kinda' like MacGyver would do*).

By cutting a one-inch diameter hole in the cardboard box you can run the tubing from the box into the kettle. To control the flow use a siphon clamp positioned on the tube one foot from the bucket. Squeeze the hose clamp into the closed position and completely open the spigot.

Now place the bucket in the insulated box and feed the tubing through the hole.

To make your beer really smooth, try steeping specialty grains no higher than 170°F.
—Edward Wren, *E.J. Wren Homebrew, Inc.*

Keep the plastic lid (and the top piece of insulation) on top of the bucket between sparge water additions to slow heat loss.

Tip 48: Super-charge your Corona mill

Does cranking a Corona mill for 10–15 minutes have you spending less time brewing and drinking home-brew? Would you like to crack 8–10 pounds of grain in *less than 6 minutes*?! Then follow these simple steps to turn your hand-cranked Corona mill into a high-speed grain grinder.

Materials/tools needed:

– Corona mill

– two 5-gallon plastic buckets

– heavy-duty plastic bag (clear if possible)

– $^3/_8$ in. (or larger) electric drill

– one $3^1/_2$ in. long ($^5/_{16}$ in. dia.) carriage bolt

– key-hole saw or coping saw

– bench-mounted vise

– duct tape

This is what you will end up with:

Your countertop-mounted Corona mill will have one plastic bucket surrounding it with two openings. One opening on the side of the bucket is to place the shaft of the carriage bolt (headless and twisted into the Corona mill) through, so you can attach the electric drill. Another opening at the bottom of the bucket enables the mill to be clamped to a tabletop and also allows cracked grains to fall through the opening. A plastic bag with the bottom cut off is attached up through the bottom of the bucket in order to allow the grains to collect in another 5-gallon bucket, placed on the floor (or in a chair).

How to build it:

1. Take the mill's hand-crank arm and wing-nut off. Attach the mill to your countertop.

2. Place bucket (open side facing up) next to the mill. With a marker draw an X on the outside of the bucket where the center of the grinding shaft lines up horizontally. Now draw about a 3-inch dia. circle around the X (see Fig. 1). Next draw a vertical cut line on the bucket, from top to bottom, through the X.

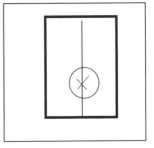

Fig. 1: Cut lines for side of bucket.

3. Turn the bucket on its side and continue the vertical line across the bottom of the bucket (see Fig. 2). Now draw two lines on the bottom to form a pie slice starting 4 inches from the edge where the side and bottom lines intersect.

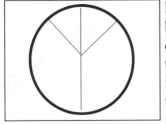

Fig. 2: Bottom view with cut lines.

4. Now you are ready to make the cuts using a coping

or key-hole saw. Cuts on the side of the bucket create two semicircles, and cuts on the bottom create two pie-shaped pieces of plastic to discard (and recycle).

5. Now spread apart the plastic bucket and wrap it around the already-mounted Corona mill. Use duct tape to tape the bucket back into its original form.

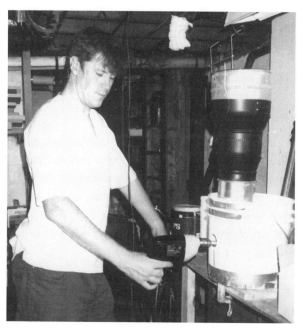

Chris Heatley and his amazing high-speed malt mill!

6. Push 2-3 inches of the bottomless plastic bag up through the opening in the bottom of the bucket. And tape the bag in place to the bottom of the bucket (over the lip of the pie-slice opening). This acts as a grain chute.

7. Position the second bucket under the plastic bag so that the bottom edge of the bag rests about 3–4 inches inside and below the top lip of the second bucket.

8. Put the carriage bolt in your vise and cut off the head. Screw the uncut end of the bolt into the mill's shaft (the threaded hole which the wing nut went into). Attach your electric drill to the other end of the bolt and tighten.

Ready to roll! Just fill up the hopper (funnel-type cylinder on top of grain mill) with grains, plug in the drill, and away you go. You may have to push the grain through the bucket opening to keep it flowing into the plastic bag. With the drill at half-speed you will be done in 5–6 minutes!

Because the hopper only holds 1–2 lbs. of grain you have to keep stopping to fill it. To solve this problem you can easily fabricate a hopper extension by putting together stove pipe reducing couplers. For example, attach a 9 in.-to-7 in. dia. reducer to a 7 in.-to-5 in. reducer which then fits in the top of your Corona hopper. (*Hopper design by Linda Fuerderer.*)

To save money you can use several empty 2- or 3-liter soda bottles. With a little cutting and duct taping you can create a really ugly (but useful) hopper extension for the price of some soda.

Ideally keep the grain mill set up permanently. If you cannot, the mill can easily be lifted out of the bucket without having to untape everything. Be sure to clean your mill, bucket, and hopper with soap and hot water periodically to keep it clean. And dry everything before putting away.

Tip 49: A soda canister chiller system

This technique can **save you half the time** it takes for chilling your wort to yeast pitching temperature using an immersion wort chiller. If you use an immersion wort chiller and you own a 5-gallon soda kegging system, you already have all of the equipment necessary.

Fill your soda keg ¾-full with cold water, and throw in several trays of ice cubes. Close the lid. Connect the tube from the liquid-out connector on your soda keg to one end of the wort chiller. Position the other end of the wort chiller (outflow) in your sink. Hook up the CO_2 gas cylinder to the gas-in connector on the keg. Now turn on the gas at 5–10 psi.

Instead of 15–20 minutes to cool the wort, it will take 7–10 minutes. Control the speed of the flow by adjusting the psi level on your CO_2 gas cylinder. *Pretty slick!*

Join a homebrew/beer club. The best tips for brewing come at our club meetings.
          – Bob, *The Flying Barrel*

Tip 50: Draft beer chiller

Homebrew to go. Build yourself a homebrew chiller (cold jockey box). Use a 10–15 foot length of food-grade FDA approved plastic tubing. Buy a small picnic cooler and run the plastic tubing in a coil in the bottom of it. Drill two holes (near the top of the cooler) slightly larger than the diameter of the tubing you are using in the plastic cooler. Then, run the tubing through the holes and connect a beer spigot to one end and a liquid-out connector to the other end. Hook up soda keg, throw some ice and cold water in the cooler, and your homebrew gets chilled as it flows through the tube.

Clean and sanitize serving tube before and after use.

— **Easy on the ice.** Be careful not to put too much ice in the cooler or else the beer line may freeze. You only need $1/4$ of a bag of ice and 2 quarts of water.

— **Five gallons too much to lug around?** Try rushing the *growler* to your next outing or party. In the early 1900s a *growler* was a small metal pail with a lid on it that would be filled from the beer tap at a local bar. Then it was rushed back home (usually by children) for their parents to drink with dinner.

Simply attach a plastic hose long enough to reach down into a plastic 1- or 2-liter soda bottle. Avoid splashing and quickly screw the cap on when it's full. If you keep your keg fairly cold, not much carbonation will be lost. *Now rush the growler!*

Appendix A

How to pour and drink a homey (homebrew)

When offering and giving out your delicious home-brew to friends and family, make sure they know how to pour and drink it. I've been to a few parties where people try drinking homebrew. But after it foams a little—or they pour the yeast sediment into their glass—the brew gets dumped or worse, ignored. (*"No. . .don't twist it. They're not twist-offs!"*)

A copy of the following steps will help the receivers of your fine gift to better appreciate it.

How to pour and enjoy a homebrew:

1. Keep upright in basement or cool place (not the fridge) before serving. Flavors and aromas come out better with a chilled—not freezing beer.

2. Use a bottlecap opener.

3. Pour homebrew slowly into 1–2 beer glasses (or a pitcher) without setting it back down until empty. These are called *one-pours*.

4. Watch toward the end—as yeast sediment starts to come towards opening, stop the pour.

5. Enjoy homebrew with friends and family. And don't forget to make a toast.

Good health and enjoy. Cheers!

Appendix B

Less confusion at bottling time!

Ever wonder how many bottles you will need to bottle a given batch of beer? What if you have different size bottles?

The following chart tells you how many bottles you will need for bottling a given amount of beer:

Gallons	——————— BOTTLE SIZE ———————			
	6 oz.	**12 oz.**	**16 oz.**	**22 oz.**
1	21	11	8	5
2	42	21	16	11
3	64	32	24	17
4	85	42	32	23
5	106	53	40	29

This information will help you to mix and match different bottle sizes within a typical 5-gallon batch. For example, you can bottle two gallons with eleven 22 oz. bottles and bottle the remaining three gallons with 32 twelve oz. bottles.

Note: It is a good idea to have one or two extra bottles sanitized in case you break one—then you will have a replacement.

Source: Newsletter of the *Kalamazoo Libation Organization of Brewers*, Kalamazoo, MI, Tom Fuller.

Appendix C

Authentic German bier pretzels fit for a Bavarian King or Queen

These soft German pretzels are served at the *New Hampshire Biernuts* homebrew club's annual Oktoberfest. Every year these pretzels are a big hit.

Ingredients:

– 1 cup warm water (105°–115°F)

– $\frac{1}{2}$ cup of homebrew (i.e., stout, porter, or hoppy ale)

– one package dry baker's yeast (or two level teaspoons of bulk baker's yeast)

– $\frac{1}{2}$ teaspoon sugar

– $4\frac{1}{2}$ cups flour (sift before measuring)

– one egg, beaten

– coarse Kosher salt

Pour water into a large mixing bowl. Sprinkle yeast and sugar over surface. Stir until dissolved. Let stand for a few minutes. Add *the* secret ingredient (homebrew!).

Put three cups of flour in a large bowl. Add yeast/homebrew mixture and part of the water. Alternate the rest of the water and flour until you have dough which can be formed into a ball.

Turn out onto a lightly floured board and knead—until smooth and elastic—for about 10 minutes.

Place dough in greased bowl, turning to grease top. Cover with a towel and let rise in a warm place (i.e., 70°–80°F) free from drafts until doubled, about one hour.

Punch dough down. Divide into 16 equal portions, about two ounces each. Form pretzels by rolling out by hand until the dough is about $1/2$-inch in diameter and 14–16 inches long. Make a figure eight with the dough with ends open. Pull each end of the dough up and over where it crosses. Then, push down where the ends of the dough rest on the pretzel, overlapping the ends by about $1/4$-inch.

Place pretzels about two inches apart on greased, foil-lined baking sheets. Brush lightly with beaten egg and sprinkle with coarse Kosher salt.

Bake at 475°F in preheated oven for 12–14 minutes or until golden brown. Remove from baking sheets and cool on wire racks. Makes 12–18 large pretzels.

Store pretzels in paper (not plastic) bags so condensation does not cause salt to melt.

Try this recipe using $3/4$ white and $1/4$ whole wheat flour.

Serving tips: Undercook pretzels by 3–5 minutes, then before serving, heat them at 400°F and finish the baking. For added decadence—brush hot butter on pretzels before serving. Have hot and sweet mustard available for dipping.

And most definitely wash these babies down with some of your tasty homebrew! If you do not have any beer ready, bring some fresh pretzels over to share with some fellow homebrewers. They will *love* you.

Prossit!

Appendix D

Bibliography of Resources

Brewers Publications. *Best of Beer and Brewing*. Vols. 1-5. Boulder, Colo.: 1986.

Brewers Publications. *Brew Free or Die: Beer and Brewing*. Volume 11. Boulder, Colo.: 1991.

Miller, Dave. *Brewing the World's Great Beers*. Pownal, Vt.: Storey Communications, Inc., 1992.

Miller, Dave. *The Complete Handbook of Home Brewing*. Pownal, Vt.: Storey Communications, Inc. (A Garden Way Publishing Book), 1990.

Noonan, Gregory. *Brewing Lager Beer*. Boulder, Colo.: Brewers Publications, 1986.

Papazian, Charlie. *The New Complete Joy of Home Brewing*. New York: Avon Books, 1991.

Zymurgy, Special Issue: Beer and Fruit. Summer 1992. Boulder, Colo.: American Homebrewers' Association.

Appendix E

Use this recipe to brew yourself a truly *great* traditional British Bitter ale.

INGREDIENTS for *Back to Basics Bitter*:

–3.3 lbs. light unhopped malt extract syrup

–3.3 lbs. extra-light unhopped malt extract syrup

–1 cup caramel (crystal) grains (60°L)

–7–9 gram package ale yeast

–⅔ cup corn sugar (for priming)

–1 teaspoon Irish Moss (20 mins. before end of boil)

–1.5 oz. Kent Goldings, 1 oz. Fuggles, and 1 oz. Cascade hop pellets

Boil time: 60 minutes

Hopping: 1 oz. Kent Goldings & ½ oz. Fuggles at 60 minutes, ½ oz. Kent Goldings & ½ oz. Fuggles at 30 minutes, and ½ oz. Cascade at five minutes from end of boil.

Original Gravity (O.G.): 1.044–1.048

Final Gravity (F.G.): 1.008–1.012

Brewer's Specifics: Transfer from primary to secondary after the head drops (3-4 days). Ferment at ale temperatures for at least 1 week in secondary. Dry hop with ½ oz. Cascade in the secondary (or make a hop tea).

Enjoy soon after bottling and aging.

Cheers mate!

So, you are a homebrewer... Now, what's the next step? Will you some day be a Pete Slosberg (former homebrewer, now *the* famous Pete of Pete's Wicked Ale)? I'll be reading (drinking) about you soon!

(Author and his homebrewmobile.)